The Seven Powers
of
Radical Loving Leaders

Erie Chapman, M.T.S., J.D.

Author, *Radical Loving Care*

President Emeritus, Riverside Methodist Hospital

Founding President and CEO, OhioHealth

Past President, Nashville Baptist Hospital System

Ideas into Books® WESTVIEW

Kingston Springs, Tennessee

Ideas into Books®
WESTVIEW
P.O. Box 605
Kingston Springs, TN 37082
www.publishedbywestview.com

ISBN 978-1-62880-078-4 Perfect Bound
ISBN 978-1-62880-080-7 Cloth with Dust Jacket

First edition, May 2015

Photo credits: Cover photo "Caregiving," by Tia Ann Chapman for the *Hartford Courant.* Other photographs courtesy The National Archives.

The author gratefully acknowledges permission to reprint quotes and small portions of other work as indicated in the text.

Printed in the United States of America on acid free paper.

Previous works by Erie Chapman

BOOKS

Life is Choices Choose Well (1995)
Radical Loving Care (2003)
Sacred Work (2006)
The Caregiver Meditations (2008)
Scotty the Snail (2008)
Inside Radical Loving Care (2011)
Woman As Beauty (poetry and photographs) (2012)

DOCUMENTARY FILMS ON DVD

"Acts of Caring"
"Sacred Work"
"The Servant's Heart"
"A Place Called Alive"

WEBLOG:

www.journalofsacredwork.typepad.com

FEATURE FILMS

Who Loves Judas?
Alex Dreaming

SHORT FILMS

Amies Nues

MUSIC CDs

Blessed Baby
The Quiet Piano
Angel Hour
Chapman Piano Concerto #1

Dedication & Thanks

Born of the sun, they travelled a short while toward the sun
And left the vivid air signed with their honour.

Stephen Spender

This work is dedicated to loving caregivers everywhere and to their leaders.

And it is dedicated to my dearest friend, William F. Banta, Esq. Bill is one of the nation's top labor lawyers. He has been practicing, teaching, writing about and advancing the precepts of excellence and leadership commitment since we were college students and law students together in the 1960s. He continues to spread the message of enlightened leadership to organizations nationwide. I love him as a brother.

Very special thanks and love to Marian Hamm, RN, MSN, Tracy Wimberly, RN, Jeff Kaplan, J.D., Steve Garlock, Frank Pandora, J.D., Nick Baird, M.D., and Mark Evans, and, in remembrance, the late Bruce Trumm & the late Reverend Bob Davis.

Thank you to each of you for the seasons when we were new
together reaching for the sky—and touching it.

Thank you to America's top Healing Hospital Leaders including: George Mikitarian, PhD, Laurie Harting, RN, Jason Barker, CPA, Bridget Duffy, M.D., Nancy Schlichting, Joel Allison and James N. Baird, M.D.

Thank you to Mitchell Rabkin, M.D. (Beth Israel Deaconess and Harvard Medical School), John Noseworthy, M.D. (The Mayo Clinic) and Toby Cosgrove, M.D. (The Cleveland Clinic) for your leadership of America's finest healthcare organizations.

Thank you David Whyte, Minton Sparks, and the late John O'Donohue for creating spiritual links among corporations, healthcare, the arts, and beauty through your gifts of storytelling, poetry, and music. And thank you, Mary Nelson, for your dedicated editing and for your wonderful support of this book.

Thank you Jim O'Keefe for your business insights and leadership charm and Cathy Self, PhD, for your frequent encouragement that I write this book. Thank you Karen York for your loving leadership at Alive Hospice and Jan Jones for leading a model of Radical Loving Care. Thank you Nancy Todd Collier, Dar Hayes, and Rhonda Swanson.

A special thank you to Liz Wessel, RN, MSN for her example as one of America's most loving caregivers and for her everyday encouragement to live love, not fear.

Special thanks to the board of Erie Chapman Foundation for their support of this work.

Thank you to my late father for his leadership example and to my wife for all the years she has spent supporting my career. Thank you to Tia and Tyler and to Miles, Sonia, Linus, and Caroline. May you always lead from love, not fear.

And, thank you to my sister Martha. She has spent her life caring for others.

Table of Contents

"Live Love, not fear."

Erie Chapman

RADICAL LOVING CARE

Radical Loving Care is God's Love expressed in the caregiving world. It means living Love, not fear. It is radical because it is exceptional and therefore rare. Only the finest caregivers can sustain it.

A Radical Loving Leader is one who practices Radical Loving Care in her or his leadership calling.

Rivers grow small. Cities grow small. And splendid gardens
Show what we did not see there before...

The features of my face melt like a wax doll in the fire.
And who can consent to see in the mirror the mere face of Man?

Czeslaw Milosz , from "Rivers Grow Small"

Slow & Deep

I am still learning.

Michelangelo's last words

For those who are truly alive, learning is a lifelong experience. Against the dictates of learning that require patient study comes the truth that every modern leader's life feels chased by the sharks of immediacy.

Beauty can only be understood at a slow pace. Because it requires reflection as well as practice, the same is true with the art of leadership.

We have time for what we believe is important. This book will speak to you if you decide you are "still learning."

The Crucial Method

Some think we can make deep change quickly. That some epiphany will transform us as completely as it did Paul of Tarsus. The brilliant Henry David Thoreau knew the truth: "As a single footstep will not make a path on the earth, so a single thought will not make a pathway in the mind," he wrote in 1854. "To make a deep physical path, we walk again and again. To make a deep mental path, we must think over and over the kind of thoughts we wish to dominate our lives."

How do you make this book worthwhile? The answer is to be a teacher as well as a student, a coach as well as a player. It is to bring joy and purpose to your leadership learning experience so that it will illuminate your life and the lives of the people who count on you.

Every study shows that we remember only 10% of what we hear, 20% of what we read and 70% of what we do. *But we remember 90% of what we teach.*

Find a fellow leader to work with. Take one of the seven principles in the book, the power of persistence, for example, and teach it to him or her. Then have them teach the same section back to you. Do this for one hour every week or at least every month. Practice the principle in real life and report back to your teaching partner.

This is by far the way to bring about the change you want to have in your life. This single practice is what transforms your leadership and makes this an exciting experience instead of just an assignment.

The Heroic Tradition

He was born in the minds of the ancient Greeks eight hundred years before the arrival of Jesus. In his time, the world fell into darkness. Zeus had removed fire from the earth. Who would be bold enough to reclaim this element and thus save humankind? Who would be the leader that would sally forth on such a mission, risking his being so that we might live?

He was named Prometheus. He was the hero who reclaimed fire and thus brought both life-giving warmth and salvific light saving us from the cold, dark punishment inflicted by Zeus.

There are several versions of this story. The one most told is that Zeus retaliated against the heroic Prometheus with the severest of punishments. First he granted him immortality. Next, he condemned him to be chained to a rock for eternity. Each day, an eagle would eat Prometheus's liver. Because he was immortal, the liver would be regenerated and then would be eaten again by the torturing eagle.

This punishment lasted for a thousand years until Hercules, another giant leader in mythology, released Prometheus from his agony. These two are part of the heroic tradition of leadership and sacrifice.

The myth of Prometheus survives as an example of what radical loving leaders can accomplish. Leaders do great things for humankind. They reshape the present and create a new future. They also risk agony at every turn. They are passionate, they have purpose and they are persistent. Prometheus, like all great leaders who flew above us across history, shows us that love calls us to our highest self.

The Stakes

All that a man has to say or do that can possibly concern mankind, is in some shape or other to tell the story of his love...

Journal of Henry David Thoreau, May 6, 1854

THIS IS A BOOK ABOUT LOVE.

All your life choices depend upon whether you chose to engage love or turn instead to a lesser power. The stakes are the quality of your life and the lives of those around you.

The Seven Radical Loving Leaders went beyond the ordinary and, because you are a healthcare leader, you are called to do the same. Radical Loving Leadership is not just a job. It is a calling to do the most important thing you were meant to do in your life. Accordingly, think of your work as meaningful or, if you are not frightened of the term, sacred.

If you treat your leadership work as ordinary your career life becomes ordinary. When you treat your work as sacred then your work life becomes sacred. The power of purpose and the thrill of meaning will energize your days.

The symbol used in this work ( ) shows two intersecting circles with a line threading through them and a heart in the middle. It suggests the three elements of sacred work. The intersecting circles show the weaving of need with love. The line threading through is the golden thread. It represents the ancient tradition of caregiving. That thread is now in your hands to hold or to break. The heart shape represents a Servant's heart.

The Sacred Encounter, the Golden thread and the Servant's Heart are the concepts that underlie this work. They are the ideas that bring meaning to you as you consider your commitment to Radical Loving Leadership.

Consider the human experience. Consider the caregiver experience. What if you were a patient in your own hospital?

At last. After a night of interrupted sleep you have finally entered a comfortable drowsiness. The alarm will ring soon. You do not want to rise yet. But, that pressure in your bladder. Get up or rest a little longer? You feel a little confused, as if drugged.

Is your son up yet? Did he finish his homework? The soft desire for more rest seduces. You remember that you have to meet with Jim today to review layoffs.

Get up or try to slip back into the slipper of sleep?

Drugged. Did you take an Ambien? You're a nurse. You should remember.

If only it were Saturday. The bladder pressure wins. You roll to your right to rise, but something is pulling at you.

The alarm goes off. You can't reach it.

The first thing you see in the dim light is an IV pole. The alarm is connected to a monitor. The news crashes over you. You are the patient. You can't get up.

The bladder pressure is serious now. You hit the call button. You wait. Three minutes. Five minutes. Nine minutes. Finally, you can wait no longer.

You hear two voices coming down the hall. "It's the old lady in 14 again," one says.

You remember that the "old lady" is you. The doctor says you've only got a few more months. Your soaked sheets attack your nausea. The nurse comes in the door.

"Where have you been?" you ask her.

"We're short-staffed here at General," the nurse says. "You're not the only patient on the fifth floor, Ma'am."

You ask yourself if any of your nurses treated patients like this when you were a leader. You know that they did. You know that you did. You wish you could go back.

It's too late.

TIME & SUFFERING

The only thing that lasts a long time is suffering.

All other time—occasions of comfort or joy—moves faster. If you are lying bedfast in the hospital and need the bathroom a five-minute wait for a nurse feels like an hour. The drilling pain of a kidney stone can convert a twenty-minute postponement of Demerol into half a lifetime. At a deeper level the horror of long starvation makes life itself an interminable hell.

Suffering in its various forms is the core reason that underlies what is a stake in caregiving. It is why Radical Loving Leadership is so desperately required for caregivers whose job is not only to cure but also to help heal.

In a way that offers more eloquence than I can muster famed *New York Times* columnist David Brooks writes that, "...the big thing that suffering does is it takes you outside of precisely that logic that the happiness mentality encourages. Happiness wants you to think about maximizing your benefits. Difficulty and suffering sends you on a different course."

What is that "different course?" Our selective amnesia can cause us to forget how much the ill need relief from suffering *now!* Pain free at your desk it may be hard to connect with the pain-flooded woman in the room two floors up and how she is counting on *you* to make sure she receives great care all the time. Our desire for pleasure causes us to discard thoughts of pain, and the experience of it, as quickly and effectively as possible.

Leadership in healthcare does not allow us this luxury. We must remember, not forget. Our own suffering ennobles us if we will allow it to do so. That is well demonstrated in the life of the polio-afflicted President Franklin Roosevelt, one of the seven leaders profiled here. The same is true of another highlighted leader. Lincoln's agonies with the Civil

War and with his own depression clearly ennobled him. Brooks writes that, "...suffering drags you deeper into yourself." He references the theologian Paul Tillich who wrote that, "people who endure suffering are taken beneath the routines of life and find they are not who they believed themselves to be."

Radical loving leadership arises from the rich and often ignored place in your soul that lives beneath "the routines of life" and beyond quotidian schedules. In order to replace current patterns with new thinking about leadership, we need to explore and reveal that ignored place and then incorporate it into our leadership life.

Years ago, on my "Life Choices" television show, a young woman shared that she was grateful for her experience overcoming cancer. To my surprise, she said she would rather have had the disease than not. Cancer taught her things. It ennobled her. I have had a similar experience across my half century with Crohn's disease. Lying on the floor cramped up with agonizing spasms I found myself slipping outside routine thinking and into a place where I not only understood suffering better but was also changed by it. It is unlikely that I could have understood the importance of my role in healthcare leadership had I not been hounded by the loneliness and terror that illness inflicts.

It is so easy for leaders to allow the layers between them and first line staff to seal them off from suffering. You are not a manager in a shirt factory. You are part of a unique organization devoted to caring for people in deep need. Staying in touch with suffering rather than running from it or papering it over is part of the way you tap the life force you need to become a radical loving leader.'

If you were a baker you might awaken at midnight wondering if you set the right temperatures on the all-night oven. As a manager of a local store you could worry if you have enough staff for next day's Memorial

Day Sale. The number of loans in default might disturb your sleep if you were a bank manager.

But what are the stakes in hospitals?

You are a caregiver. Everyone in a hospital is one. If you are a doctor you may awaken wondering if you called in the right orders. You wonder if the patient will live.

What if you are the nurse manager for the fifth floor? You wake up at 2 A.M. remembering that you had to cut staff. Last week, Judy was handling six patients. This week she is handling ten. But, that's not our fault. You were ordered.

How will you answer Judy's complaints? No one trained you for this. You're guessing a store manager has had more leadership training than you have. Your guess is right.

Every job is important. But, where are the stakes higher—in the bakery or in the hospital—at the local store or in the hospital—in the bank branch down the street or in the hospital?

At 2:20 a.m. this morning a new life entered this world in a delivery room at Baylor Medical Center in Dallas. Over the next minutes an old life left this world at Beth Israel Hospital in Boston.

What are the stakes inside the walls of Baylor and Beth Israel today?

A half hour later at The Mayo Clinic Hospital in Minnesota and Parrish Medical Center in Titusville, Florida nurses transferred critically injured people onto Emergency Room gurneys. At 8:00 a.m. at Presbyterian Hospital in Albuquerque, The Cleveland Clinic, Henry Ford Hospital in Detroit and at Mercy General in Sacramento surgeons will begin repairing damaged hearts.

What are the stakes for the critically ill? If you are a patient in one of the hospitals mentioned you are lucky. They are among the best. But what if you are elsewhere?

> *There's so little asked of you; after a while / you forget that you're using half of yourself.*
>
> Stephen Dunn

Today, at an unnamed hospital in Chicago and another in New York two different Vice Presidents will sit in meetings, review boring agendas and complain there are too many meetings. They will do nothing to change that. One of the VPs started his career as a physical therapist. The other began as an accountant. Their professional training was excellent. Their leadership training amounted to a week's instruction from their previous bosses and a two-day seminar on leadership at the local Marriott hotel.

Both VPs have been using less than twenty percent of their team's potential and about the same of their own. Both have received good reviews even though employee and patient satisfaction in their areas is below the 50th percentile. Today, each will email a list of immediate layoffs to their Human Resources executive.

At the Chicago hospital it is the last day of employment for Lucy Thomas, a twenty-year nurse and single mom. She will remove the 4 x 6 photo of her fourteen-year-old son from the break room bulletin board, put it in her purse and take her last walk to the parking lot with two other nurses also laid off.

Tomorrow, one of their elderly patients, Ellen Jackson, will fall and break her hip. Her family lawyer will claim there was not enough staff to look after her. One month later she will die of pneumonia. Her children will grieve the pain that their mother lived in her final days. Lucy Thomas will wish she could have been there to help.

WHAT ARE THE STAKES
IN HOSPITAL LEADERSHIP?

The needs in caregiving are not ordinary. They are radically important. That is why the word "radical" appears in Radical Loving Leadership?

Why the word "loving?" Radical need requires radical love.

Caregivers need Radical Loving Leadership. The stakes are that high.

How will you learn to move from good to radical in your leadership? Rilke wrote that, "For one human being to love another... is the most difficult task of all." Perhaps that is why so few leaders reach success. It is hard enough to love the people you live with much less the people you work with.

Will you unwrap your potential or leave most of it unopened? On your last day of work and last day on earth will you be able to say you met your life's highest challenge and lived love?

Ignazio Silone framed a truth volcanically in *Bread and Wine*: "We live the whole of our lives provisionally. We think that for the time being things are bad, that for the time being we must make the best of them and adapt or humiliate ourselves, but that it's all provisional and that one day real life will begin."

Every moment holds the chance to begin living your life anew. Alternatively, we can go through the motions. Perhaps, you see that around you—people who have given up or perhaps have never tried, or have tried and given up.

We have all witnessed it. "We prepare for death complaining that we have never lived," Silone continues. "Sometimes I'm haunted by the thought that we have only one life and that we live it provisionally, waiting in vain for the day when real life will begin. And so life passes by..."

This challenge is great news for those willing to embrace a new path! *The Seven Powers of Radical Loving Leaders* promises you the chance to live your "real life" by using the same seven energies all great leaders have used.

Start today.

If not now, when?

WHY SEVEN?

The grouping of life energies in this book into seven powers (all starting with a "P" as a memory aid) is both arbitrary and important. Yes, it could have been five powers or eight. It is also true that you can take any number and make it into something. I chose seven because this number has had an important significance over history.

For example, there are seven wonders of the world (not eight or six) seven days of the week (not five or nine.) In Judaism, the seventh is a day of rest. In Hinduism there are seven chakras, or centers of energy. In the Catholic Church there are seven virtues and seven deadly sins. The virtues are a combination of the four cardinal virtues from ancient Greek philosophy: prudence, justice, temperance, and courage, combined with the three theological virtues described by St. Paul of Tarsus in his letters: faith, hope, and charity (Love). Some argue there are seven colors in the rainbow, seven seas, seven planets (including the sun) and seven precious gems.

Seven is as good a number as any and better than most. It is a way to organize our thinking around natural forces that express themselves through our hearts and into our lives. If you are a contrarian, you can rearrange them as you wish. Just be sure and notice them. One way or another, these seven powers of loving leadership are the source of all of the positive energy we have available to us.

AN UNCERTAIN SUN

Every beginning is opaque. It occurs in a nest that is hidden below the light.

John O'Donohue

Once upon a time, when I was four years old, I awoke in the night feeling sick as a dog. A California moon reached through my bedroom window but it brought no comfort. I ran to the bathroom and threw up.

As I leaned into the loneliness of nausea I felt a hand on my shoulder. "You'll be okay, Chip," my dad said.

Suddenly, I felt reassured. My father was sharing the isolation of my illness with me. His calming hand and voice delivered relief.

It was one of the first experiences I can identify in which I remember feeling loved. When you are well, you can feel bullet proof. From the height of your health, you may even condescend, unintentionally, to those who are ill.

When you are sick illness looks endless.

In the depths of your pain, comfort appears out of reach.

Caregivers bring hope.

Your life experiences have arrived in a caravan of moments. But, your love for life grows from a single belief: that each day is worth living.

When you were a little kid, who cared for you when you were sick? Why do you care about caregiving?

How did your mom show her love? You may recall a cold night when she stroked her warmth across your face. What you know is that the love your caregiver gave you when you were sick was as important as any medicine.

Love lived in my mother's lap. The sheets she cleaned and tucked were ever white. She was ever young.

As you recall your earliest days, you recollect what mattered most. It matters most today. It is love.

You are walking through time with your life on the line.

How high are the stakes in your life? How high in healthcare?

When you or someone you love is deathly ill you understand the stakes. Amid pain nothing seems more crucial than relief.

LARGE STAGE, SMALL STAGE, RIGHT STAGE

Vacation. It is one of the most loved words in any vocabulary.

This morning, from a small stage seven floors up, I survey a large stage named the Atlantic Ocean. The sun paints the sky an impossible blue. A fine wind billows the white dresses of a double-masted yacht. Three motor craft slice the waves. Jet skis captained by teenagers bounce along.

A freighter floats at anchor a half mile from shore. Hundreds vacation on beach towels.

If this were one of those coastal days where the sun blinks through the clouds one minute and storms attack the next. If hurricanes occasionally crashed the beach wreaking havoc and lightning struck in deadly ways, literally. If most days were clothed in the clouds graying the flat lands of Ohio and fluorescent lights lit linoleum lined hallways, then it would more accurately reflect most of my life experience.

This is likely true of your life as well. You have won victories and suffered defeats. In between, you lived a string of days that may often have seemed ordinary.

You may also have dreamed big when you were young. You have noticed those among you who ascended from small stages to large ones.

The famous fascinate. As children, we read stories of Lincoln or Mother Teresa or Martin Luther King and wondered if we were like them in any way.

You watched a popular singer, tested your voice in the shower and wondered if you could win the acclaim the way she or he did. Did you later dismiss those dreams as childhood fantasies? What hopes replaced your wish for stardom?

As your life walked its own path some voice within you may still have asked, "What do stars have that I don't?" Maybe talent? Maybe luck?

Luck and talent may have won fame for some. However, fame never makes anyone a true success. Some stars may not even have been *that* naturally talented anyway.

After Barbara Walters was picked by ABC News to become their first female news anchor she was asked how she became an instant success. "*Instant* success?" she said. "I've worked my butt off for twenty years. I got this job because I'm persistent."

Indeed, no one thought Walters, with her well-known difficulty in pronouncing certain words, would become one of the best-known television personalities in history.

Meaning matters most, not fame.

Hard work hues true success.

The child of illiterate parents in Somalia who works her way to the United States and goes to college is no "instant" success on graduation day. My father-in-law was literally (like Lincoln) born in a log cabin with a dirt floor. Both his parents died when he was six years old. He was farmed out to relatives.

Twenty years later he was practicing medicine. When he became president of The Wisconsin Medical Association he was not thinking to himself that his success was either "instant" or easy.

Stardom does not matter much. Helping others does. The Somalian college graduate who became a nurse understands suffering. That knowledge fortifies her compassion. The log-cabin-born doctor delivered babies and saved lives in operating rooms. Both lived meaning.

Forget about talent and luck. Both are out of our control. The giants of history can teach each of us how to make our lives meaningful regardless of luck or talent. They prove that *you can access the same seven powers they did.*

It is not arrogance to compare some of our leadership success to Lincoln's or daily caregiving labors to Mother Teresa's.

It is smart to learn from the greats.

Look to the big stages and learn so that you can illuminate all the colors in the spectrum of your life.

Meanwhile, what is it we seek when we ask for the autograph of a movie star or a sports king? When we stand next to them in a photograph are we somehow hoping our proximity will make us great as well? That their fame will rub off?

Over the years, as my life story unrolled on the usual small stage, the great stars in the constellation of history seemed unreal. Still, because the famous were accessible I studied them. The point of studying history is not just to memorize but also to apply learning.

Leader learning can start early. As a high school student I recorded the televised Nixon-Kennedy Presidential Debates and press conferences on my dad's reel-to-reel tape recorder. At night in bed, I played the tapes back and imagined how I would answer questions.

Churchill's speeches played through my ears at Deering Library when I was at Northwestern University. Lincoln's law career inspired me in law school.

As a trial lawyer asking questions and as a hospital CEO answering them in employee meetings I tried to transfer the learning from the big stages of history onto the small ones I occupied. Thus, a little light from the bright stars shined into courtrooms and hospital cafeterias.

Some of the greatest stars I saw practiced nursing or led operating room teams or taught history or led in hospitals. What intrigues is how much more meaningful our own work can be if we study history and learn to engage the seven particular universal energies.

The seven universal powers are:

Purpose, passion, potential, persistence, positivity, presence, and peace.

You have every one of these. Expand how you use them.

None of these energies is grounded in raw talent or luck.

They are in the air all of us breathe.

Joel Allison, CEO of 36,000 caregivers at Baylor Scott and White credits God for every bit of his success. To enter a winning partnership with God, Joel had to apply the gifts God offers to each of us.

Neither Joel nor I, nor Henry Ford's Nancy Schlichting nor any other leader profiled offers himself or herself as ideal models. The purpose of sharing stories is that ancient hope we all share: To learn from each other.

Share the light of their loving leadership as we hike together through the mysterious forest called leadership.

The players in the early drama of my life were clients and the stage was a courtroom. For decades after that, a cast of heroic and average caregivers, capable and indifferent board members, a mix of fine and foul physicians and a vast humanity of very sick people populated my life.

The stages were the villages called hospitals and these people were their citizens. You live most of your waking life in one of these towns perhaps, more than you do in your home. The stakes are life and death and suffering. The rewards come when sick citizens leave feeling healed.

To whom do we go when pain and disease flood our bodies? Where do blaring vehicles transport us when we are flooded with pain or felled by disease? Where do we flee with our most massive needs? We enter the arms of the people you lead. We trust our lives and our sacred health to caregivers.

If your mother were sick, would you trust *every* caregiver you manage to tend to her?

If you take care of the people who take care of people, your staff will take great care of your sick mother or your ailing child. If you demean the people who take care of people, they may demean the patients who trust them.

There is no higher greater power than love. There is no greater calling then loving care. The stakes are never greater then for those who command caregivers.

That is you.

Since hospitals occupy the acreage of birth and death we trust doctors and nurses and every kind of therapist to search out and destroy the diseases that invade us. We count on them to drive back the pain that grips our souls.

Why do you lead? How do you lead?

You work beneath an uncertain sun. As you know so well, behind the best weather a cataclysm may lurk. How do you prepare your heart as well as mind?

> *Remind yourself.*
> *Nobody's built like you.*
> *You design yourself.*
>
> Jay Z

Even if you are fulfilling the promise of your best gifts you may wish to improve. I have quoted mid-nineteenth century essayist Henry David Thoreau more than any other in these pages because his writings best inform the practice Radical Loving Leadership. For example, he wrote, "The mass of men [sic] lead lives of quiet desperation. What is called resignation is confirmed desperation." Is that is not true of you is it true of some of those you lead?

What if you celebrated the lives of your finest caregivers even more? What would happen to productivity? Have you found the courage and grace to retrain the worst caregivers or to send them out the door so they will not cause more suffering?

It takes more than the energy of a good wind to sail well. You must, of course, have a fine crew. The best captains engage positive energy. The worst drift inattentive and survive only in calm seas.

Good news. The seven powers of loving leadership are here to help. They are grounded in the greatest power on earth. It is love, not fear.

How much of your life is lived in fear?

How much in love?

Legendary leaders have been assembled to teach you how to engage your best leadership. One of the seven has been singled out to show you each power and demonstrate how they engaged it to succeed.

You do not need to be a heroic figure to lead successfully. Yet, in Joseph Campbell's book, *Hero with a Thousand Faces*, he offers language that may help you see your leadership journey in a new light:

> *The dogmas of the quiet past are inadequate to the stormy present.*
>
> Abraham Lincoln

"A hero ventures forth from the world of the common day into a region of supernatural wonder: fabulous forces are there encountered and a decisive victory is won: the hero comes back from this mysterious adventure with the power to bestow [many benefits] on his fellow man."

None of us are heroes, yet heroes are all around us. Some remarkable stories dotted the landscape of my leadership experience: suicides, two murders, a hostage-taking at gunpoint, and all of that happened in just my first year as President of Riverside Methodist Hospital in Columbus.

These larger dramas teach. But we learn more from the "small" stories.

Why lead to the status quo? That is not where the treasure hides. If the present is "stormy" you cannot succeed using only yesterday's tools.

Loving hospital cultures are places where peak clinical excellence and financial performance are the norm. These are the places loved by employees, visitors, the community, doctors and the banks that lend them money.

Pioneer through enough frontiers and you will suffer wounds as well as victories. You will also blaze new trails.

Everything has some meaning. Only a handful of things in our life hold radical meaning. You decide whether your caregiving leadership holds radical meaning or is just a job.

You decide who to follow and how you lead. Remember that tyrants think they can make you go wherever they order you even if your goal is personal and lives in your heart. Tyrants cannot control you without your permission.

SAVING LIFE AND STEALING IT

Tens of thousands of spectacular physicians practice their sacred profession every day—awakening in the middle of the night to save our lives or ease our pain. They have spent years studying difficult texts and practicing their skills relentlessly. I have the most profound respect and admiration for the dedicated doctors and other direct caregivers who spend their lives caring for the sick and wounded. Hospital environments are inherently difficult. Leaders must do more to celebrate these heroic people.

Drs. Hector Johnson and Mike Scando. Here are two of the kind of doctors who can give medicine a bad name. Their actions signal how high the stakes can be. Both doctors were on the less-than-stellar medical staff at the first hospital I led in inner city Toledo, Ohio. For obvious reasons their names have been changed.

At 8:02 A.M. on October 17, 1977 Dr. Hector Johnson opened the mouth of Sarah Sanders and slid in a tube. The tube would carry the oxygen she needed when her anesthetized lungs relaxed their normal breathing.

Sarah was about to undergo a standard hysterectomy. Thirty-nine years old, she had decided that six children were enough.

The gynecologist's scalpel hovered over Sarah's belly ready to make its first incision. He and two operating room nurses waited for Dr. Johnson to complete the intubation and for Sarah to dip beneath sleep's waves.

In the waiting room forty feet away, Sarah's husband glanced at the clock. In another hour or so he could join his wife in the recovery room.

There is a basic anatomical truth that every nurse, doctor and respiratory therapist knows. The trachea leads to the lungs. The esophagus leads to the stomach.

Did you ever cough because a few drops of water "went down the wrong throat?" Then you know the important difference between the door leading to your stomach and the one that leads to your breathing chambers.

Doctor Johnson pushed the oxygen tube through the wrong door. Soon, Sarah's stomach began to fill with air. While her lungs collapsed her belly rose.

"Dr. Johnson. You put the tube in the esophagus instead of the trachea," a nurse pointed out.

Dr. Johnson ignored her. She repeated her warning.

"I'm the doctor and I know what I'm doing," he shouted.

Finally, the gynecologist joined in. "Hector, you've got the…" He never finished the sentence. The patient went into shock and arrested.

The frantic dance of cardiac resuscitation began. Paddles were placed on Sarah's chest. I remember hearing the "Code Blue" announced over the public address system.

The Chief Nursing Officer entered my office at noon. "We lost a patient in the OR this morning," she said.

I was thirty-three, six years younger than Sarah. How did the caregiving system I oversaw breakdown? Who would hold Dr. Johnson accountable? What else did we need to say to Sarah's husband?

EVERY DAY RISKS
WHEN THE STAKES ARE HIGH

Dr. Mike Scando was also a popular obstetrician at Toledo's Riverside Hospital in the 1970s. He delivered more babies than the next three OBs combined.

Some would say protocols were looser back then. Dr. Scando managed to breach even those softer guidelines.

A year after Dr. Johnson killed Sarah Sanders Dr. Scando's negligence almost resulted in another death. The use of Pitocin delivered intravenously to initiate labor was common in the 1970s and is still used in many hospitals today.

I am advised that delivering Pitocin at a high drip rate can cause the pregnant patient to experience "titanic" contractions, a phenomenon that can become so violent that the patient can hemorrhage and die. Rules required that doctors administering Pitocin at a high drip rate must be present in the hospital at all times.

Dr. Scando thought he was above those rules. He would sometimes start Pitocin drips and leave to deliver a patient at another hospital. Nurses complained. The medical staff formed a wall of protection around Dr. Scando and refused to act.

It was time for the administration to intervene. I waited too long.

On a June day in 1978 Dr. Scando introduced a Pitocin drip into the veins of Mary Kendrick. He then left to deliver a baby at St. Vincent hospital two miles away. Minutes later, Mary suffered violent contractions and began to hemorrhage. Only prompt and effective intervention by delivery nurses and a nearby doctor saved Mary's life.

What can a lay CEO do? The Chief of the Medical Staff, Dr. "Mulroney," not only protected Dr. Scando but he nominated him to be Chief of Obstetrics.

I told Dr. Mulroney that the board would block Dr. Scando's appointment and that Dr. Scando should be suspended, not promoted.

Dr. Mulroney threatened to "have my job." He told me he would start a rumor that I was having an affair with the nurse director of obstetrics.

"You know that's a lie," I told the Chief.

"Of course," he responded with a smirk. "But, everyone will believe it."

As soon as he left I called an emergency staff meeting and told the staff the plan for dealing with the Chief. "To try and stop me Dr. Mulroney is going to spread the rumor that I am having an affair with

Shirley (Shirley stood up and said, "NOT true!" Everyone laughed.) "So when you hear the rumor you know it's false," we said.

This pre-emptive step was effective. The rumor that went around was that Dr. Mulroney was a liar.

Over the next three months a battle ensued among the board, medical staff and administration. Ultimately, Dr. Mulroney was forced to resign as Chief of Staff. Dr. Scando was never appointed Chief of Obstetrics. He did, however, continue to practice.

> *The heart is stronger than you think.*
>
> Beyoncé

Why do leaders often lack courage? They fear being fired. It is so much easier to ignore trouble or to buck the problem over to someone else. Healthcare needs loving women and men who tackle the tough problems head on.

Why is your leadership important?

Lay leaders can directly affect medical care. Cultures of peak performance drive the best care.

Fortunately, physicians like Doctor Johnson, Dr. Mulroney and Doctor Scando are much less likely to practice today. Still, tragic errors and ineffective medical staff leadership continue to plague some of America's hospitals. The best self-correct.

Why are so many television dramas and movies located in courtrooms and hospitals? They are places where important things happen.

Why is it so critical that you develop the strength and the talent to guide others? Caregivers, and the patients they attend to, are counting on you to ensure safety and quality.

I agree with Beyoncé. Your heart is stronger than you think.

You also understand that humor can strengthen your leadership. A friend of mine shared that when she had a cold her father would make Bananas Foster and set it on fire. She would laugh and she felt better.

Make the Bananas Foster. Set it on fire. Let laughter carry you through some of the suffering you see every day. Let your heart embrace your real life now and every day to come.

Live love, not fear.

Part One

The Problem

Why Things Must Change

QUALITY OF LIFE

> *There is no illness that is not exacerbated by stress.*
>
> Allan Lokos,
> *Patience:*
> *The Art of Peaceful Living*

When noise is determined to be more than just an irritation, good leaders alleviate it. When leaders accept that short staffing causes patients pain, then new solutions flow.

When leaders begin taking better care of the people who take care of people, caregivers release the power of their love and the human experience improves.

Make a picture of what best care looks like. Lead your organizations into that picture. Imagine that your mothers will be coming for care at the hospitals you run.

What about our mothers? Can we be sure they will be well cared for in the hospitals and hospices and nursing homes where we work?

THE BIRTH OF THE MOTHER TEST SM

Meet Dr. "John Silver." He was one of the finest orthopedic surgeons at Nashville's Baptist Hospital. In 1998 his clinical results were excellent and he was respected as a talented technician.

Shortly after I became President and CEO Dr. Silver approached me outside the doctor's dining room.

"Erie, this loving care stuff you've been talking about is nice but how is it going to help my patients? If someone has a compound comminuted fracture of her right leg then the leg needs me to fix it. The leg doesn't need loving care," he said.

"But, the leg is connected to the person and the person needs loving care," I answered.

He looked skeptical so I persisted.

"Dr. Silver, what if the patient was your mother?"

His face softened. "Well, of course, I would want loving care for her."

"Isn't every patient someone's mother or sister or child or friend?" I asked.

Dr. Silver became so transformed by that encounter that he changed his whole practice. Thus, he became not just a technician but also his best self.

THE SINGLE BEST SOLUTION TOOL

That encounter with Dr. Silver led to the single best tool to solve the biggest problem in healthcare: *The Mother Test.*

> *The natural state of motherhood is unselfishness.*
>
> Actress
> Jessica Lange

The problem is that too many hospitals, leaders, and caregivers are failing The Mother Test. This means you cannot trust them to ensure loving care for your mother.

THE TEST: If your mother (or someone else you love) was admitted to *your* hospital how confident would you be that *each and every caregiver* would treat her in the way you want her treated?

If you lead a caregiver who you don't want touching your mother, why are they on staff?

Solution: The leadership solution is to create a culture where everyone passes The Mother Test—where all caregivers, male or female, practice the "motherhood of unselfishness."

THE LEADER TEST

The Mother Test instantly births *The Leader Test.*

If caregivers are failing, that means that leaders are failing.

Ordinary need requires nothing radical. Radical need calls for radical love and radical loving leadership

It should be obvious (although it is not) that most people were *not* meant to be leaders. This includes many who are leading right now—promoted out of their most natural role into one they were not meant to do.

Fortunately, there are millions of first line associates who love their work and do it well. They are the ones every leader relies on and must honor.

But there are others who should be neither leaders nor caregivers. Look at your team right now. Do they live love in their caregiving? Again, if *you* are leading people that cannot pass They Mother Test *why are they there?*

If you are *not* taking the steps necessary to ensure great care for patients than are you truly a successful leader? More bluntly, do you deserve the job?

Be clear that this test applies to *every* leader in the hospital whether they supervise direct caregivers or not. Leadership in housekeeping, maintenance, security and dietary, for example, impacts the safety of caregiving environments.

Leadership in human resources and finance are further examples that impact the quality of both the patient and associate experience.

MORE ON THE PROBLEM OF SUFFERING

It seemed like it tuck (sic) a long time for freedom to come. Everything just kept on like it was.

Mittie Freeman, former slave

The first sharp pains assaulted his chest in the middle of the night.

Frightened, struggling to stay calm, my friend, Azaz, tried hard to convince himself he was not having a heart attack. But after several hours of intermittent chest pain he called his doctor's office, described his symptoms and asked for an appointment.

"The doctor is booked for the next month," the receptionist told him.

"Well," Azaz said, "In a month I may be dead."

He got through to his doctor who sent him to the nearest hospital, a for profit institution just beyond the hem of Nashville. A cardiologist was supposed to tend to him but did not appear.

Azaz was hooked up to monitors. He stayed all night, and all the next day, and all the next day.

Each night he tossed and turned—awakening at the noise of overhead paging and nurses coming to take his blood pressure and temperature

Each day he waited for the cardiologist. But no doctor of any kind *ever* appeared.

Doctor-less his anxiety continued to rise. "I felt like my heart was a time bomb waiting to explode," he told me.

On the fourth day, a nurse entered and asked my friend, "Are you the heart attack?"

"I'm still waiting to find that out," a startled Azaz answered. "I thought *you* would tell me if I had a heart attack."

"Well, you probably did," the nurse said, "but the monitors have not been working so we don't know for sure."

Later that day, things got worse. The Christian chaplain appeared and asked Azaz, a Moslem, how he wanted religious services to be handled should he die in the hospital.

"I felt like I was about to receive last rites," he told me.

After four days of indifferent, incompetent and potentially deadly care Azaz was transferred to Nashville's St. Thomas Hospital where he finally got the attention he deserved. The next day, triple bypass surgery was performed, probably saving his life.

Back at home months later Azaz noticed that the never-appearing cardiologist at the first hospital had submitted a bill for $14,000. His insurance company paid it.

One way to justify ignoring a human being is to address them by their diagnosis. To the staff, Azaz had no name. He was "the heart attack."

Another way to mistreat patients is to be a cardiologist who never visits. A third way is to utilize a broken monitoring system. A fourth way is to have a chaplain who starts planning funeral rites for a patient that has not even received a diagnosis. And I have not even mentioned a fifth mistake—the doctor's receptionist who was prepared to make Azaz wait a month for care of a likely heart attack.

One error on a patient might be explainable. Five errors on one patient is outrageous. Would *you* want *your* mother cared for in such a hospital?

Caregivers are caught in the wrong kind of system. The recent history of healthcare leadership does not reflect well on us. Not unlike former Mattie Freeman, it can feel like "a long time for freedom to come" to our beleaguered organizations. Your leadership is so much more important than you may think it is. Our work can be freighted with meaning or we can choose to drift along on the stale winds of the routine.

A RADICAL NEW DEFINITION OF SUFFERING

> *America's health care system is neither healthy, caring, nor a system.*
>
> CBS news anchor
> Walter Cronkite

What happened in Azaz's body when the receptionist told him he could not see the doctor for a month?

How was his health affected by the long delays?

What happened to his blood pressure when the nurse named him "The Heart Attack" and informed him that the monitors on his chest had not been working?

Did he suffer when the chaplain suggested it was time to make arrangements for his possible death?

All of these questions beg another one: What does it mean to suffer in a hospital?

Look at the importance of being loved through the caregiving eyes of Mother Teresa: "Being unwanted, unloved, uncared for, forgotten by everybody, I think that is a much greater hunger, a much greater poverty than the person who has nothing to eat."

Consider the eighty-five year old patient who has been lying on a gurney in your hospital for an hour. People walk by her but do not see her. How cared for does she feel? How much suffering is involved in the task of waiting?

All of this work, and the answer to passing The Mother Test, can be summarized in one, four word phrase, Live Love, not fear.

Physicians at Harvard-affiliated and Yale-affiliated hospitals and at the Cleveland Clinic are finally learning new answers about suffering. They are documenting, through new Chief *Experience* Officers what has been obvious to millions of patients for years.

Suffering has been wrongly limited to medical pain. It turns out suffering is more than the discomfort from an incision or the soul-splitting agony of a migraine headache.

In an article in *The New York Times* (February 17, 2015 authored by Gina Kolata) Dr. Kenneth Sands, Chief Quality Officer at the highly regarded Beth Israel Deaconess Medical Center, reports that, "suffering, whether from long waits, inadequate explanations or feeling lost in the shuffle, is a real and pressing issue."

When your bladder fills and you cannot empty it because you are bedridden, a slow response to a call light can be agonizing.

When you are desperate for sleep because you are sick, a public address system or loud noise from the nurse's station causes suffering.

The very experience of putting on a patient gown can drape your soul in humiliation—another kind of suffering.

A caregiver can raise or lower your heart rate and blood pressure simply by how she or he enters the room.

A rude admitting clerk can aggravate the anxiety you already feel just by *being* in hospital.

A doctor who refuses to listen to you or look you in the eyes can cause unnecessary suffering as well.

"Unnecessary suffering" is the key phrase. So many of the bad experiences that ruin your hospital stay can be avoided. Much better, they can be converted from demeaning moments to healing experiences.

Doctors are finally recognizing the health impacts of communication. For example, your doctor blurts out, "Oh, it looks like you have cancer." Or you lose a valuable, like a wedding ring. "These are harms," Dr. Sands said. "They elicit suffering. They can be long lasting, and they currently are largely un-quantified, uncounted, unrecorded."

Vanderbilt Medical School physician and professor Roy Elam and University of Michigan Professor Daniel Moerman contend that "the placebo effect" should be renamed "the meaning effect." Too many people discount the impact that so-called placebos have on physical health.

Instead of dismissing placebos as useless sugar pills, they believe we should be asking why placebos are so often effective. They understand that positive and negative language and interactions directly impact health, suffering and healing.

The responsibility to improve patient encounters rests on the shoulders of leaders. In addition, bad leaders cause their subordinates another kind of

> *Every patient visit*
> *is a high-stakes interaction.*
>
> Dr. Thomas Lee, M.D.

suffering. Poor leaders create stressful work environments. Absenteeism often rises.

Leaders need to improve the human experience for all. Physicians like Dr. Sands and Dr. Thomas Lee at Press-Ganey are on the right track.

"Every patient visit is a high-stakes interaction," Dr. Thomas Lee opines. "It is a big deal for the patient and it is a big deal for you. And all you have to do is be the kind of physician your patient is hoping you will be."

When leaders define suffering too narrowly they lower the importance of patient satisfaction. Thus, it does not get the attention it needs. They need to establish definitions of care that include *all* hospital-caused suffering.

Meanwhile, most leaders are not taking good enough care of their staff. And some CEOs are not yet clear on the need to transform bottom-line obsessed organizations into cultures of caring.

Expand your definition of suffering.

DOCTORS AS PATIENTS

After twenty-five years as a physician a friend became a hospital patient for the first time. "I was shocked," he told me. "It's terrifying to be stuck in a bed twenty-four hours a day! I hated being on the other side. My favorite caregiver was a housekeeper. I looked forward to her visits every day."

I asked another veteran physician how his wife had been treated during a stay in an Intensive Care Unit. "Two nurses saved her life and two almost killed her," he said angrily. "If I had not been by her side, she would be dead. I'm stunned."

How does it feel to be a patient? Sometimes, veteran caregivers forget.

The problem? Our caregiving system is not only broken. Our leadership system has lost its way. Poor accountability, an excessive focus on profits, short staffing and government style bureaucracy are damaging the patient care experience.

Consider the leadership of Jesus, Mohammed, Moses and the Buddha. All of them taught using stories. Religious leaders, business leaders, and politicians rely on stories to win followers; why not us?

Very few people turn on the television to watch a lecture on C-Span on how to be a better leader. Instead, we watch movies, read books, and play games that stir our energy, relax us and fuel our dreams and our imagination. In fact, people connect most with stories where they can identify with a main character.

Learn to tell stories. Teach with stories. Lead using stories. Invite your colleagues to tell stories that value what you wish to promote.

You are the main character in your own story. Remember that your partners are the main character in theirs. Keep this in mind when you are seeking their support.

WHEN SMALL BECOMES BIG

Things that are very small to the healthy can loom large for the sick.

Carole Williams had nothing to laugh about on the morning she awoke with no feeling in her feet. She and her husband Stu went to the doctor.

After examination his face bore the grim expression no patient wants to see. "You have Guillain-Barré Syndrome," he told Carole.

Was one of your childhood nightmares to be completely paralyzed, unable to speak, drowning in your own body?

That is the future Carole's physician described. "The numbness in your toes will rise up your legs. In a few days you will be paralyzed from the waist down. Next your upper body will numb. Then, you will be unable to move except, perhaps, to blink."

The good news about this terrible affliction is that most patients recover. But, Carole's next year was agonizing until one afternoon a therapist appeared offering brief freedom.

"We are going to place a device in your throat," the therapist said. As you exhale, you can say one sentence. Let me know when you are ready by blinking your eyes."

She blinked. The device was inserted.

Her husband waited anxiously. Which of the thousands of wishes his wife had bottled up would pour forth?

Carole exhaled her sentence. It sounded to Stu like, "Gedamihrablegeeblau."

"Are you trying to say you love me?" Stu asked.

Carole blinked no.

"Are you trying to say you love our kids? Again, Carole blinked a no.

"Let's try again," the therapist offered.

This time, Carole sputtered three words, *"Get my hairdresser!"*

When patients are bedridden small things become big. Great caregivers understand.

But soon after this incident Carole's body pivoted towards health (Subsequently, she experienced a ninety-nine percent recovery.) Did laughter tip the scales?

Carole and Stu tell and retell this story. Each time, they roar with their audience about that magic moment when laughter illuminated their darkest hours.

Sometimes a hairdresser can be a healer as well as a nurse or doctor.

THE PROBLEM OF PITY

There is a cellular difference between Radical Loving Care (RLC) and so-called Tender Loving Care (TLC.) They are like different molecules.

RLC is God's Love expressed in the caregiving world. It means living Love, not fear. It is radical because it is exceptional and therefore rare. Only the finest caregivers can sustain it.

Fortunately, Radical Loving Care doesn't expect perfection. It recognizes the rich and difficult shadows in life as well as the light. Because you exist by nature at the center of your own consciousness it takes work to recognize how you are balancing your needs with the needs of your fellow beings.

When you are fearful, your needs dominate your ability to live Love. At your best, you transcend your needs to relieve the suffering of another. This is the challenge of Love. There is nothing more important. Radical Loving Care means living Love, not fear.

TLC, at its best, is the expression of kindness that flows from compassion: your ability to empathize not just sympathize.

Compassion and pity are opposites. One trite but true saying is that, "Pity stops and stares. Compassion stoops and cares."

Pity condescends to suffering. Compassion meets suffering heart to heart.

A person expressing pity says to a patient, "I feel so sorry for you." A person expressing compassion says to a patient, "This must be so hard for you. I want to help you in any way I can."

The pitying person feels superior to the suffering one who is "lesser than."

Compassion looks eye-to-eye.

The compassionate caregiver recalls his or her own suffering to appreciate the agony of the patient.

RLC calls for competence and tough-mindedness *as well as* compassion and a tender heart. Never call it "that touchy-feely stuff" because it includes competence!

Adopt Radical Loving Care, as have tens of thousands. You and your staff will pass the most important test caregivers face.

> *This time 'round I'll be a giver*
> *I have saved me long enough.*
> *I will dig down to the bottom*
> *and I'll fill me right back up.*
>
> Darrell Scott,
> *This Time Round*

When your leadership gains radical meaning you will celebrate those you want caring for your mother, you will retrain Mother Test failures and you will remove those who do not belong at your mother's bedside.

No one can pass the test one hundred percent of the time, but every fine leader and caregiver delivers peak performance most of the time because every fine leader lives love.

WHAT IS BROKEN?

In 2014 a 52-year old woman was admitted to a Nashville area hospital with severe lung problems. Four months later she was still there and that is where she died. A few months later her husband received a copy of the bill for her care submitted to the insurance company. It totaled $1.3 million dollars.

In general Americans receive excellent health care. In many other ways, our health care system has been broken for decades. The way we know our leadership system is in radical need of improvement is to look at how many bad patient and caregiver experiences happen each day and night. Again, too many leaders ignore the suffering *among their associates.*

This is not just a case of medication errors, falls and botched surgeries. It is a matter of the inhuman way we are often treated by a system that can demean and degrade us both as patients and as caregivers.

The broadest responsibility lies not in the lap of either patients or caregivers. It sits at the feet of leaders that tolerate mediocrity.

If leaders take care of the people who take care of people they will transform the human experience. Hospitalization will become healing for *all* concerned.

THE PROBLEM WITH THE HUMAN EXPERIENCE

Caregiving leadership is about managing the entire human experience. Patient care that lacks competence harms patients. Patient care that lacks compassion causes suffering as well.

Competent leaders love caregivers. Incompetent leaders harm their caregiving staff and damage patient care.

Leaders who are kind but incompetent cause as much trouble as those who degrade and terrorize.

HOW SOCIETY AND SYSTEMS CAN DEHUMANIZE

Sustaining humanity amid an increasingly hard world requires constant effort. At age six, little Glenn came home from school. He walked about the house looking for his parents. The house was empty. Glenn's mother and father had abandoned him.

From age seven to age fifteen Glenn lived in nineteen different homes; shoved from place to place like a chicken thrown from cage to cage. At fifteen, Glenn ran away and moved into a cardboard box outside a factory.

By eighteen, life had degraded him deeply. The first thing he said to me through prison glass in Tennessee's Death Row was, "I don't trust you

> *The same organizations we need to help us must not demean us.*

because I don't trust anyone." Trusting no one, Glenn had made his own efforts to undermine the society he believed had trashed him.

Civilization does not tolerate what Glenn did in 2001. At twenty-eight, he was convicted of a double murder. He was sentenced to death and entered prison; a place where he will spend the rest of what *he* calls "his god-damned- sorry-ass life."

Eighty-six men and one woman live on Tennessee's Death Row. We call them murderers. Glenn, the man I have ministered to for three years, may have killed in part because his own childhood was murdered. Nevertheless, he is responsible.

As his minister, I see Glenn not just as a body with a number but a person with a life story. Glenn's story illuminates his humanity.

In many ways, he would like his story to end, to be ushered down the hallway to "get the needle." When I walk through each of the eight gates between the outside and the hell that is Glenn's cell I tell myself I am ministering to a human being.

Murder is not to be excused but may be explained. Those among us who kill must be sealed off from society. But society dehumanizes itself when it dehumanizes people.

That is the problem with prisons. They are supposed to incarcerate, not humiliate.

It turns out that dehumanization can be the problem in any of society's institutions including government agencies, big companies and hospitals. The same organizations we need to help us can demean us.

PRISONS, HOSPITALS, AND THE POWER PYRAMID

Physician Don Berwick has done more to lead improvements in hospital safety than has any other modern leader. One of the ways he was able to accomplish that was through his deep understanding of the power pyramid in healthcare and who is at the top. In 2010 he addressed a new group of power holders in his commencement speech at Yale Medical School, "...today you take a big step into power," Berwick said. "With your white coat and your Latin, with your anatomy lessons and your stethoscope, you enter today a life of new and vast privilege."

Berwick wanted to warn new doctors of the risk that comes with power. It is, of course, arrogance. Unintentionally, power can distance the power-holder from the humanity and vulnerability of both the weak and what some leaders sadly describe as "the lower level employees."

There is an even greater threat to our humanity. A new icon sits in the throne atop the pyramid. It is technology. Margaret Hamburg, M.D., warned of this risk in an appeal to Stanford Medical School graduates in 2012 "Patients do not put their trust in machines or devices," Dr. Hamburg said. "...the more dependent on technology you become—the easier it becomes to lose your humanity, forget your compassion, and ignore your instincts."

Nurses also hold sway in the power paradigm. At a recent graduation ceremony at Duke's School of Nursing Duke professor of cardiology Dr. Robert Califf warned graduates that if we ignore "the fundamental nature of *human caring at the gut level*, we may develop a more efficient system, but it won't be better."

In their struggle to please board members and doctors and to hit budget targets powerful leaders are increasingly inclined to value power and money over purpose and mission. The best way to redesign our broken healthcare system is to place love at the top of the hospital hierarchy.

Before I entered healthcare leadership in 1975 I was a federal prosecutor. Within a week of becoming an executive at Riverside Hospital I noticed a striking (though unintentional) similarity between hospitals and prisons.

❖ Prisoners are stripped of their clothes, given demeaning uniforms, numbered, and placed in cells with complete strangers.

❖ Patients are stripped of their clothes, dressed in demeaning outfits called patient gowns, are numbered, and then placed in rooms with complete strangers.

❖ Prison visiting hours are controlled. Patient visiting hours are controlled.

❖ Prisoners are subjected to interruptions that occur at the convenience of guards. Patients are interrupted in the middle of the night for tests.

❖ In prison, guards hold power over inmates. In hospitals, caregivers hold power over patients.

❖ Patients living in the customized comfort of their homes and families are suddenly occupying sterile centers populated by strangers.

None of these comparisons is meant to insult caregivers. They highlight a *system.* Prisons and hospitals operate on hierarchical power models that can unintentionally push people into a power model that can be unhealthy.

The best hospitals are solving this problem.

The worst keep repeating the mistakes of the past.

You are likely working in a hospital that is somewhere in the

> *McDonalds is introducing a Big Mac clothing line...*
> *It's called a hospital gown.*
>
> Comedian Conan O'Brien

middle, a mix of very enlightened and sometimes condescending leaders and caregivers.

Again, primary responsibility rests in the hands of well-paid top leaders. The system relies on them to do more, to get out of their offices and apply the solutions that have already been proven to work.

THE PROBLEM OF FEAR BASED LEADERS

Six months into my role as CEO of Nashville's Baptist Hospital I discovered something about our Chief Nursing Officer. "Ellen" was a thirty-year veteran of nursing and very competent. She told me she supported my message of loving leadership. One day I discovered otherwise. One of Ellen's directors was talking with me when her pager went off.

"Oh no!" she said, her face turning white. "It's Ellen's extension."

"Why is that bad?" I asked.

"Every time I see that extension number I get a stomach ache."

> *Power based on love is a thousand times more effective and permanent than the one derived from fear of punishment.*
>
> Mahatma Gandhi

Later that week I approached Ellen. "Your staff is afraid of you," I told her.

"Good," she answered honestly. "I want them to fear me. Otherwise they won't obey me."

Remember that patient satisfaction was below the 70th percentile and employee satisfaction was worse. Nursing, as the largest group, also has the biggest influence on patient satisfaction. Turnover in nursing was in the upper teens.

Ellen is an honest, high integrity individual. Her approach was simply different from mine.

We arranged a good retirement for her. As far as I know, she believed our action was reasonable because as an honest individual she could see her old approach would clash with our loving care philosophy.

At another hospital I spoke with Chris, a mid-level director and James, a veteran Senior VP on a leadership team that included two high-control leaders. Why do financial officers need to be loving caregivers? Alice, the CFO, so terrified her staff that they were afraid to make a move without checking with her. "She has the worst human relations skills I've ever seen," James said about his colleague.

"Alice works seven days a week and drives her staff mercilessly," Chris chimed in. "That has not helped our financial performance one bit."

The same was true of the Chief Operating Officer. Jane-Ann keeps "an enemies list," Chris said. She punishes any of her staff that criticizes her. Turnover among her leaders is terrible.

"Her staff spends their time guessing what Jane-Ann wants," James said. "That is a huge challenge since Jane-Ann frequently gives confusing directions and often changes her mind."

In both cases, the CEO refused to replace these energy-sucking leaders. The hospital continues to be a sub-par performer. Remarkably, this same CEO told me one day, "If you look at how we are performing I guess I would have to give myself bad marks." Two years later, the "marks" are not much better yet the same guy is in charge.

In order to lead to the standard of The Mother Test you need to be, in Martin Luther King's words, "tender-hearted as well as tough minded," compassionate as well as competent. Ellen's style leaned so far to the tough end of the spectrum that she could never have guided her nurses to the loving standard we sought to establish.

The best Chief Nursing Officer I worked with was Marian Hamm at both Riverside Toledo and Riverside Methodist in Columbus. When she retired, I put Tracy Wimberly in charge of patient care at Baptist and she hired Kim Fielden. Free of daily fear, morale soared and so did productivity. Soon, our patient satisfaction rose to the high nineties and turnover came down to the single digits. Financial performance also rose sharply.

This is the power of loving leadership in a caregiving organization.

STATUS QUO LEADERS – MANAGING TO BE AVERAGE

Interestingly, Marian was recently admitted for care to a large Ohio hospital. While waiting on a gurney to be transferred into her room, a sign on the wall caught her eye. "Congratulations, team!" the sign read. "We have reached the 72nd percentile in patient satisfaction!"

> Listen, are you breathing
> just a little,
> and calling it a life?
>
> Mary Oliver

"When I was in school, 72 was a 'C,' just average," Marian told me. "Why would I want to go to a hospital where the people taking care of me are just average? I wanted to be in the kind of place we led. But, they don't have one in this town."

After she was discharged she told me, "It was just like the sign said. I had some good caregivers and some terrible ones, including one who told me he could not refill my oxygen when the tank ran low because it was against policy for him to go get a tank. In other words, I would give them a C."

I worked with another hospital whose patient satisfaction had been stuck around the 68th percentile for four years. When I began consulting with them I asked them their goal. "The 72nd percentile," they told me "We want to be a little above average."

Imagine telling that to friends, "Come to our hospital. We are a little above average."

Later that month the CEO informed me that one of his employees had complained that the 72nd percentile was too aggressive. "We're doing okay," the employee told him. "Why are you pushing us?"

One large (but shrinking) hospital I consulted with was stuck in the mud of the ordinary. Some signs of mediocrity were obvious. A small sticker pasted at the main entrance to the hospital proclaimed that the mission of the hospital was to insure that patients had a "safe" experience.

Nothing is wrong with that mission as far as it went. Safety is crucial and many hospitals have been failing that test. But that was *all* the statement said.

Patients do not come to a hospital only to be safe. They come seeking cures and healing.

But there was something worse. None of the several leaders I asked knew about the statement on the front door. Second, the hospital had been cutting staff to the point where safety was more of a failed question than a successful answer.

In fact, staff cuts had reached such low levels that dozens of nurses were responding late to call lights by telling distressed (and innocent) patients, "We're short-staffed."

What kind of confidence would you have if you were a patient in a short-staffed hospital? Furthermore, what are you, as a bed ridden being, supposed to do about the nurse's short staffing complaint?

Imagine telling your mother: "Come to XYZ General. We're short-staffed."

By definition most hospitals are average. This means that most people are allowing their doctors to admit them for treatment of serious illnesses to an average organization hoping they will somehow receive above average care!

Average hospitals deliver *average* care to people who need *best* care.

More and more leaders are insisting on "A" level care. Isn't that what you would like for your mother especially if she has a life–threatening illness? *The Seven Powers of Radical Loving Leaders* offers a map to "A" level care.

HARD QUESTIONS

> *...the biggest determinant of staff satisfaction is how team members feel about their leader.*

What *is* your story? How do you lead? Ask yourself what your team thinks of you, not what they say but what you know is true.

Look at your team. Know that each one of them is *watching you* like a hawk. All day every day each member of your team evaluates what your signals mean to their jobs.

Every organizational study proves that the biggest determinant of staff satisfaction is how team members feel about their leader. Every breakthrough team has a visionary leader.

Historically, hospitals have not always been a rich breeding ground for visionary leadership. Instead, they are often cumbersome organizations that may operate more like government agencies than innovative enterprises.

Hospital CEOs have a tough job. They are called to balance competing voices of doctors, employees, board members and the community. Accordingly, hospital leaders are often rewarded for maintaining stability, not exploring change.

Comforted by big salaries and buffered by layers of boss-pleasing managers there is a great risk that top healthcare leaders will be seduced by the status quo. Hundreds of CEOs talk about big change then act so small that nothing happens.

These well-meaning CEOs speak change because they know patients need it and because it sounds good. Meanwhile, they know that there are too many caregivers in their organization they would *not* want looking after their mothers. But, they also know that if *their* mother were admitted they could guide her around "the bad ones" and into the hands of "the good ones." Why worry about the patients of *other* people's mothers so long as yours is okay?

You may be comfortable in *your* job. Why rock the boat?

Today, leaders need to infuse the caregiver experience with radical loving leadership. The stakes have become too big for status quo leadership.

Medicare is monitoring patient satisfaction at every hospital in the country. Continued sub-par performance can result in penalties. It is this threat that has got some bosses realizing that if they "play-it-safe" *they* may suffer as well as patients.

A simple bit of leadership psychology proves why ordinary leadership is dangerous. Retail selling is an important job, however, caregivers are not retail clerks selling shirts and dresses. Since the patient is not paying for the healthcare product then why should a nurse care about "customer service?" None of them were trained that way and most find it demeaning to classify sick patients as customers.

Nurses are caregivers, not salespeople. They need to be motivated by enlightened leadership, not mass marketing.

In order to move the average caregiver into a zone of peak performance CEOs need to establish cultures of high excellence where *only the best is acceptable.* When they tolerate caregivers that fail The Mother Test they fail their responsibility to patients and the community.

> *Probably in the not far distant future we will crawl out of our old methods of education, as a snake sheds its skin, and re-organize a new plan.*
>
> Dr. Charlie Mayo
> Co-founder, Mayo Clinic

Oft-cited examples of Mother Test success in health care include ones I have mentioned: The Mayo Clinic and The Cleveland Clinic. An average performer at the Mayo Clinic would be seen as a peak performer in most other hospitals. The Mayo brothers were pioneers because they knew the "old methods" were outdated.

You do not receive a pass just because you are not at the Mayo Clinic. Your challenge is to innovate and inspire where you are; to win and create success in *your* arena.

THE PROBLEM OF NEGATIVE ENERGY

The sun never made it through the clouds on September 20, 1999. When I awoke that morning my memory brought me news that would snatch one of those clouds from the sky and drape it over my spirit.

One minute into the day I felt my energy sinking. This likely happened to you on that very same morning in 1999.

What kind of information could make your energy weaken? What news would give more Americans heart attacks on that morning than on any other day of that week?

The answer? September 20, 1999 was a Monday.

That news, all by itself, is an energy–sucking fact. There is a restaurant called TGIF—Thank God It's Friday. There are no places I know that are called TGIM—Thank God It's Monday.

More people have heart attacks between seven and nine A.M. Monday morning than on any other day of any week.

You may say you love your work. But it is un-American to claim you love Monday more than Friday.

I thought about this on that September day. I was President and CEO of Nashville's five-hospital Baptist Health System. I loved the job and had fought hard to get it. Why would I hate a Monday?

An obvious fact struck me: There will be a Monday every seven days. Why throw away one-seventh of my life hating a day that was certain to arrive every week?

I resolved to start loving Mondays. That means a need to love life itself and that is the process that leads to joy.

Yet loving Mondays (along with *all* the rest of life) remains a tough challenge. It requires re–thinking long established patterns. It means swimming against the tide.

To change that or any other pattern requires that you *prioritize* change until the new pattern is in place—that you move your attention thus releasing the flow of energy that comes with positive thinking.

Later in my career, someone shared one of the best sentences I have ever heard. I repeat it often. Apply these words and change your life: *Where attention goes, energy flows.*

Physically, there are plenty of energy drinks out there starting with coffee. Moving your body around creates energy. Sitting still for too long brings lethargy. The right type and amount of food supports good physical energy, the wrong does the opposite. Alcohol and drugs stimulate energy or step on it. Rest is a great basis for energy. Breathing well is crucial to energy. Shallow breaths bring fatigue and even chest pain.

But spiritual and emotional energy are the most important fuel for leaders. Think of ways your brain chemistry, the source of your moods, changes based on external events.

Put your primary energy on a driver that cut you off on the highway and you will raise your stress level. Your energy will raise your heart rate and blood pressure. Your galvanic skin response will go haywire. Acid will pour into your stomach.

Why? You chose to put your energy on a threat. After the rude driver heads off, that negative process continues. It may even intrude on your thoughts later in the day kicking up some of that same poison you felt when it happened.

NEGATIVE TO POSITIVE

Where attention goes, energy flows.

I first noticed the impact of negative thinking in a high school football game when I accidentally jumped off sides. The coach pulled me out and shouted at me: "Do that again and you are benched."

Scared, I tied a piece of string onto my facemask to remind me not to go offside. Soon I was back in the game. As the quarterback shouted the signals I stared at that piece of string. To my complete amazement, my body jumped forward prematurely. Offside again.

Sitting on the bench I wondered how that could be? How could I jump offside when I was specifically telling myself *not* to do that?

Forty years later, I got the answer from a psychologist: "It's a neuro-linguistic truth," he told me. "Tell yourself *not* to smoke and you will think about smoking. Tell yourself not to make a mistake and you increase your chance of making that mistake. The brain can't interpret the "no." *You have to turn no into yes.* Tell yourself *Yes.* I want to be healthy and you are less likely to smoke."

Of course, I sensed this as a trial lawyer. When the judge instructs a jury to ignore a defendant's sudden confession they are sure to focus on exactly that.

Thoughts and words affect brain chemistry (and, to an uncertain extent, vice versa.) Brain chemistry impacts how you feel and the quality of the energy that surges through you.

In spite of this, caregivers are constantly warned not to do wrong things instead of being encouraged to do right things.

THE PROBLEM OF MISTAKE~FOCUSED CARE

Medicine is, naturally, problem-oriented. This in itself can be a problem, causing mistakes instead of solving illness.

Put your attention on *not* making a medication error and your chance of making that error increases. Focus your attention on giving your patient the best care possible and you will more likely give the patient the right medication.

It is more effective leadership to tell your staff "We need to maintain a safe environment" than it is to tell them *not* to break safety rules.

THE PROBLEM OF DOCTOR PRESENCE

What kinds of attention do nurses and doctors give to patients? Eye contact is one of the ways we honor the person before us. Thomas Moore writes that as far back as the sixteenth century Paracelsus told doctors, "The physician should speak of that which is invisible. What is visible should belong to his knowledge, and he should recognize illnesses...But this is far from making him a physician; he becomes a physician only when he knows that which is unnamed, invisible and immaterial, and yet has its effect."

Today this insight is often dismissed by doctors as the placebo effect. Instead, it is a phenomenon that is critical to healing. To appreciate the role of meaning in healing physicians must be present. But, presence and patience are chronic issues for harried caregivers. A Harvard study shows that doctors typically interrupt their patients within the first eighteen seconds of an encounter.

> *When a doctor refuses to acknowledge a patient he is, in effect, abandoning him to his illness.*
>
> Anatole Broyard.

When *New York Times* writer Anatole Broyard was a cancer patient he expressed universal wisdom. "If he could gaze directly at the patient, the doctor's work would be more gratifying. Why bother with sick people, why try to save them, if they're not worth acknowledging?"

That is why I never liked the doctor's dictate: First, do no harm. The statement should be: First, live Love, not fear.

If doctors do that, they will treat patients with competence and compassion.

Want to become a more effective leader? Pay attention to the sources and uses of your energy. Notice your power to impact your energy and that of those you lead.

Consider what happens to your team's energy when you walk into the room. Do they feel better or worse?

The seven powers of loving leaders are about positive energy. Notice that not a single one of these high-purpose leaders was a tyrant.

Tyranny is ineffective because it insults. Love honors. Shouting surgeons increase the risk of errors. Loving doctors honor their OR teammates and achieve better results.

Tyrants control. Loving leaders trust. Abraham Lincoln understood this. He wrote, "The worst thing you can do for anyone you care about is anything that they can do on their own." If you have picked the right team, learn to trust, not control.

Your staff members are trained adults. They need the encouragement of your support. Look over their shoulder all the time and you will cripple their best energy.

Steven Covey recommends "release management." Become a coordinator who unites your team and adapts their power rather than a controller who kills positive energy. Leadership is too complicated for micro-management.

Nurture, don't nag.

High **purpose** brings positive energy. Low purpose and fear-driven leadership pours poison on the servant's hearts of your staff.

Passion awakens the greatest power on earth—Love. Desire is driven by fear. Passion can be satisfied. Desire cannot.

What is your **potential**? You have far more than you think you do. Every example of a great leader proves that.

> *...genius disdains a beaten path.*
>
> Lincoln

What is the power of **persistence**? It is the single biggest determinant of success.

Why does every great leader focus on the **positive**? Positive energy releases hope. Negative energy drains hope.

What difference does a loving and focused **presence** make? Energy moves to where you are present and flees when you are absent.

Where does the energy to deal with crisis and sustain balance lie? It lives in **peace** within, not from without.

Energy is there even when you think it is not. Imagine you are exhausted. Someone asks you to take out the garbage. You feel you cannot sit up much less perform a task. "I'm exhausted," you say. "I can't do another thing."

Four words can instantly convert your exhaustion to jump-up-in-the-air joy. The four words? "You won the lottery."

Cultivate the seven powers and integrate them. You will win the lottery of your life—the lottery that really matters—your success.

Where attention goes, energy flows.

GETTING REALISTIC.
THE PROBLEM WITH PERFECTIONISM

You are already working hard. It may sound like you are now being asked to do more. Instead, you are invited to work in a way that is both more effective and more rewarding..

Medical care imposes terrible burdens of "perfection" on every caregiver. This work asks for both competence and compassion but not perfection: Self-compassion as well as compassion for others and forgiveness as well as focus.

What is clear is that caregivers who practice Radical Loving Care enjoy their work much more. We all need rewards, and not enough caregivers and leaders are receiving *new and refreshing* kinds of recognition for their hard work.

Psychologists from Harvard to Stanford know that for rewards to work, they must not only be frequent but varied. If you receive the same kind of thanks after a while it can become meaningless.

Radical Loving Care offers its own thanks. Once love is better understood there is less reliance on the shifting sands of outer affirmation and more trust in inner rewards.

If the problem for you is lack of feeling appreciated, help another in need today and do not wait for thanks. The fact that you helped is beautiful recognition. Extra thanks, should they come, are just icing on the cake.

THE CHALLENGE MEN FACE IN CAREGIVING

It is not surprising that women make up roughly eighty percent of America's professional caregivers. The mothering instinct was implanted at birth.

On the other hand, my fellow males still make up more than eighty percent of hospital CEOs. "You have to be secure in your manhood to embrace radical loving care," a fellow CEO told me in 2003 after my first book was published.

Those "secure" males are the ones who learn to embrace love as the core element in caregiving leadership. They are the only ones who engage radical loving leadership. That is why secure men like George Mikitarian, Jim Skogsberg, Joel Allison, Toby Cosgrove, Jim Hinton and Jason Barker succeed.

THE BURNING "WHY"

Everyone thinks they want answers. But it is always the questions that matter most. Leadership gurus think the best questions start with "Why?"

Does your energy burn with a great "why" or are you simply burned out?

Arcing across more than a century and into your eyes comes a crucial bit of wisdom from Frederick Nietzsche "He [or she] who has a Why to live for can bear almost any How."

How you hear your "why" determines your life energy and how you work. Every caregiver knows that unused muscles atrophy. Every day you fail to use your spiritual muscle your earthly soul atrophies.

When people have no burning "why" they fall into mindless patterns. Their hearts fade in the tepid waters of the status quo. It is the leaders' job to swim forward, not to tread water.

"Towering genius disdains a beaten path," Abraham Lincoln wrote. "It seeks regions hitherto unexplored."

You and I may not be "towering geniuses," but do we want to live our lives never exploring what might have been? Loving leadership starts when you become a pioneer as well as a settler, "a pilgrim on life's journey."

THE THREE WORKMEN

In the old story three workmen are laying bricks. A passerby asks the first worker what he is doing. "I'm paid to lay bricks and that's what I am doing—laying bricks," the man said.

He asks the second man who says, "I'm building a wall."

The third worker replies proudly, "I'm building a cathedral."

Each answer reflects a legitimate explanation. Why is the third bricklayer likely to work the hardest and do the best job? Laying bricks holds meaning. Building a cathedral promises radical meaning.

The third worker has defined his purpose, his "why," in the most meaningful way. He has a "why" that burns in his heart and soul, as well as in his bent back.

What is your burning why? What energizes you each day? Is it your desire to provide for your family? It is your passion to help others?

Author Rob Bell tells you, "We are created with a drive to self-transcend, to move beyond oneself for the joy and blessing of others."

What help does this offer you in your life journey? Perhaps you have not yet found your burning why. It lives within you and it is the most powerful source of your best energy.

So the best energy for success derives from the best answer to the question "why?" Why work so hard? Why aim so high? Why focus on excellence?

The answer is clear and inspiring: your patients are counting on you. So are their families. So are your co-workers.

If all you are doing is laying brick because you are paid for it then burnout is not far away.

Sadly, most healthcare employees are doing just that and many are burned out. Exhausted by long hours and short staffing, led by uninspiring bosses and employed by an organization that has no vision that matters to them, they plod forward day after day struggling not to get fired.

So many caregivers suffer in work conditions that could be so much better. They cannot answer all the call buttons and all the emails and all the overhead pages in the way that is needed. They cannot handle all the questions and the constant fear of mistakes.

So many leaders struggle to solve problems they have not been trained to solve. Mentally and emotionally they thrash about trying to meet budgets and improve quality with limited resources. They, too, are afraid for their jobs.

My heart breaks for anyone who comes to work afraid. Your heart should break for their patients.

You can help convert cultures of fear into gardens of love and excellence.

THE PROBLEM OF VISION FAILURE

Organization failures can often be traced to CEOs who have failed to develop visions that matter to *everyone* in the organization, especially first line caregivers.

> *Only a "burning why" can bring out your best self.*

A collapse of vision infects an organization with a performance killing malaise. Caregivers and leaders walk through their jobs out of fear and duty lacking the centerpiece of energy: hope.

Some CEOs have hijacked the caregiving mission and replaced it with a focus on bottom line financial performance. We need good financial stewardship. But, obsession with the bottom line undermines the value of caregiving. As two-time Democratic Presidential nominee Adlai Stevenson said, "We cannot afford to be penny-wise and people-foolish."

Caregivers attend people on their first day of life and on their last and through what may be incredibly painful chapters along the way. The whole organization supports this. Housekeepers are keeping the place clean to prevent infection as well as to maintain neatness. Plumbers maintain a setting where lives are saved. Accountants support the system that insures everyone is paid.

Why is caregiving crucial? If a clothier puts the wrong garment in your bag the solution is to return it. If a nurse gives you (makes you buy) the wrong medication the result may be deadly.

Former staff and board say the two biggest keys to my success were to champion an inspiring vision for all and to focus energy on one idea: to take care of and *affirm* the people who take care of people.

❖ Want high patient satisfaction? Take care of your staff.

❖ Want excellent clinical results? Take care of your staff.

❖ Want great financial performance? Take care of your staff.

❖ Want to succeed as a leader? Pick a great team.

History demonstrates how well this approach works.

A CASE IN POINT

In 1994, ten–hospital OhioHealth (the organization I founded in 1984) employed eleven thousand people. Across that year, we had eight hundred job openings. Turnover was less than 8%. An executive in Human Resources told me that thirty thousand people applied for those eight hundred openings.

Even if that number was way high, the point is that thousands of competent and compassionate people wanted to work in a place that was known for its nationally ranked culture of excellence—a place where the number one goal of leadership was to take care of the people who took care of people.

Each caregiver working for OhioHealth was doing more than just "laying bricks." Obviously, not everyone was positive, but many saw themselves as "building cathedrals" not just doing a job.

What if you could work in a setting you enjoyed so much that you looked forward to Mondays? What if you had a boss you both liked and respected?

How would you like to spend your career in a hospital with a top-notch childcare center, a grocery ordering station in the middle of the parking lot, and a dry cleaning pick-up service?

In short, how would you like to live your work life in one of "the top ten most employee friendly workplaces in America?" (Source: ABC News Special "Revolution at Work")

Execute the principles described here and you will transform your workplace into more than an associate-friendly environment. You will create a culture of excellence that will draw the most patients and the best doctors to a place that will truly live out its mission of caring.

We were not put on this earth to give half an effort. You did not become a caregiver in any part of a hospital or hospice so that you could give average care.

If you sense you are living your days in the half–light, what would it take for you to leave the shadows; to enter the fullness of your best self?

Your life is a gift shop. Go inside and pick what you wish. Some things cost more than others. Everything has value.

ANSWERS HIDDEN IN STORIES

What is the secret of finding your burning "why?" Part of the answer is found in stories of caregiving both good and bad.

Everyone I know is enchanted by sentences that begin, "Once upon a time." These four words offer their own invitation to explore some of your finest gifts.

Stories can also become a call to action. Often, stories of mistakes and indifference teach as much as the stories of success.

Some stories of bad patient care are difficult to believe. But, you know that they happen.

THE CHALLENGE OF CULTURE

In subtle ways, the leadership culture in the hallways of power has paralleled the path of a white-male-dominated America.

As a European-American male, I look at the landscape of hospital and healthcare leadership and see meeting rooms filled with people who share my racial and national heritage more than they share the heritage of the multi-cultural staff they lead. America's hospitals are still, for the most part, run by white men.

This will and should change. Good boards of directors, currently dominated by white men, will prioritize this issue and diversity will finally arrive in America's hospital governing bodies.

White men like me were raised with Beethoven and Rachmaninoff, not LL Cool Jay or Gloria Estafan. We can be out of touch. That is why I have added quotes from contemporary stars to add to the words of Lincoln and Churchill.

White men like me read the literature of Dickens and the poetry of Emily Dickinson. We admired the Dutch Master painters not, sadly, the artifacts and traditions of Africa.

Beyonce may not be Mother Teresa. But many more listen to her than to the Nobel Prize-winning nun. Pop icons often affirm the wisdom of great leaders in their own words.

Most of us grew up Christian and do not know enough about staff who are Jewish, Muslim, Buddhist, or Hindu. Successful leaders will lean into the new amalgam of culture, not tilt away from it.

THE PROBLEM OF THE ABSENT ARTS

Spirit of Beauty. . . where art thou gone?

Percy Bysshe Shelly

All of great art is an expression of love's beauty. Engage art and marry Love. But, how do you find beauty along those linoleum-lined hallways? Where is it in the glare of fluorescent lights? "Beauty, where art thou gone?"

A central challenge of loving leadership is balance. Franklin Roosevelt and Martin Luther King cultivated the arts. Churchill painted. You can do this every day from your home and in your work.

Hospital leaders often ignore the arts in the workplace and thus cut you off from some of life's beauty. How do you balance the sterile atmosphere of most hospitals with integrating the arts?

"I have seen the grimness that sneaks into the face of the caregiver healed by music and vulnerability," Bruce Cramer, an ALS patient said in a National Public Radio interview.

Why do we need art in healthcare? My colleague, retired Senior Vice President and Chief Nursing Officer Marian Hamm, wrote a prose-poem that begins "There never has been a good day in a hospital..." This is, of course, because there are so many sick people there.

Cedars Sinai, one of the great hospitals in the nation, has benefited from rich gifts of art and the energy of the Judaic tradition. They have a superb collection of paintings and sculpture and both are displayed prominently.

You, however, are invited to do more. At Riverside Methodist Hospital in the 1980s and 1990s we offered The Oliver Wendell Holmes lecture series to all staff.

> *A beautiful thing, though simple in its immediate presence, always give us a sense of depth below depth...*
>
> Frederick Turner

Guided by Susan Quintenz, programs offered authors, artists and professors to audiences of doctors, nurses, leaders and housekeepers. Great music filled The Susan H. Edwards Auditorium, otherwise dominated by leadership meetings and medical staff grand rounds.

The best guide I know on balancing the arts and beauty is David Whyte's brilliant book, *The Heart Aroused.* Years ago, my friend Minton Sparks handed me a copy of John O'Donohue's book, *Beauty.* Taking these two books to heart can change your life.

Why block off caregivers from the healing legacy of artists and musicians? Integrate the arts into your work. Balance medicine and management science with multi-cultural presentations of film and music.

Invite a rap musician or a jazz saxophonist or a modern dance group to perform at a meeting or retreat. At Parrish Medical Center and previously at Baptist Hospital and Riverside Methodist a pianist played in the hospital lobby. Establish meditation gardens flooded with flowers.

Limn your heart with love. Celebrate beauty.

THE STUNNING IMPACT OF PEER POWER

Every leadership psychologist says that the greatest impact on the culture you occupy each day is peer pressure.

Peer power determines quality at The Mayo Clinic. Enter that culture and you will be pushed by your peers to practice "The Mayo Way," an approach that emphasizes high competence and deep compassion. The Cleveland Clinic has "The Cleveland Clinic Way."

If you had joined the NASA team that put a man on the moon or the 1980 Olympic Hockey Team you would have been energized each day by both the positivity and the sublime presence of every other member. If you switched from American Airlines to working for Southwest Airlines you would immediately feel your spirit fly.

But peer power is much bigger than that. It teaches you to adapt to the culture around you or you will feel the punishment a group imposes: shunning.

Culture determines the expression of evil as well as excellence.

The Germans are a fine people—as loving, competent and caring as the citizens of any other nation. How could such a large number of them have joined the Nazi nation? How was their sadistic side mobilized to torture and kill Jews, Poles, gypsies, Catholics, Lutherans, and anyone else they deemed "inferior?" How could that nation of noble people fall for the idea that they were a "race" so superior to all others that they could murder and maim and rape at will?

The clearest answer is that Germans of the time yielded to peer pressure driven by stark fear. They looked around at their neighbors and friends and saw them wearing swastikas and hanging red and black flags out of their windows. They did what some of us might have done. They copied them.

Germans of the 1930s and '40s saw their friends and neighbors and millions of strangers raising their arms in the Nazi salute. Turning their backs on Love they raised their arms in the same salute. Those who didn't were arrested.

What drove some people to turn in any friend that opposed the Nazi's? Fear. Many betrayed members of their own families. It was all driven by a toxic culture of soul-killing terror. A similar phenomenon grabbed the throats of the Japanese during the same period, silencing dissent.

Across the English Channel, a different peer group, led by a radical loving leader, prevailed. On the other side of the Atlantic a culture of freedom and democracy determined the daily behavior of Americans and Canadians.

Peer power excellence dominates many hospitals. The peer problem of mediocrity saps love at many others.

THE FULL POWER OF
THE RADICAL LOVING LEADERS

Every great leader engaged every loving power. Each was flaw-touched as well as light-flooded.

Every one advanced a high purpose. Each lived with passion.

Every one lived their full potential. They were all persistent. Each nurtured hope in the hearts of millions.

> *A leader is best*
> *when people barely know he*
> *exists. The people say,*
> *"Amazing!*
> *We did it all by ourselves!"*
>
> Lao Tzu
> *Tao Te Ching*

Every one of them offered a laser presence to their followers. And each one had a sense of inner peace that brought them serenity amid the storm.

Some accused the loving leaders of being egocentric. But they were actually *other*—centric, risking their lives for the common good of others.

It is the fear—driven leaders, the little Hitlers of the world, who are uniformly egocentric. High control leaders think they know it all and you do not. They use force to force-feed their egos. They threaten out of ignorance, failing to recognize that every unnecessary command disempowers their followers. They engage fear, threats and intimidation because it looks like the quickest way to solve problems.

There is one exception. In true emergencies, the need for quick action may require one person to take control. Indeed, high-purpose leaders, including physicians acting in emergencies, know how to take control and when to release it.

But, these circumstances are far less frequent than most imagine. High-purpose leaders understand that the rest of the time leadership calls for patience.

When leaders command from a place of love they also act with a tough-minded approach. They are simultaneously tender-hearted, and this makes all the difference.

To lead well stitch each of the seven powers into the garment of your life. Wear the garment each day.

These seven powers are free, but not cheap.

Listen to Oprah: "I know for sure that what we dwell on is who we become."

Think of your life as holding seven gifts.

Unwrap them.

Dwell on them.

Celebrate love.

THE DANCE OF PHYSICS

You do not need to be Lincoln to learn from him. You do need to live like Mother Teresa to engage the energy in her spirit. You do not need to dress like Gandhi or demonstrate like Martin Luther King in order to become a leader who will change the world for the better.

As she arranges flowers by the window of her country home a great soprano practices an aria. She pauses by a vase of roses to sing a particularly high phrase. Nearby, a crystal glass shatters.

Glass, like all objects, has its own vibrational energy. In that shattering encounter, the vibrations of the soprano's voice engaged the air molecules around the glass and rearranged its structure.

Leadership magic encompasses physics. Inspiration illuminates energy.

John O'Donohue describes the interplay of physics and leadership. "There is a kindness in beauty which can inform and bless a lesser force adjacent to it," O'Donohue writes in his masterful book, *Beauty*:

> *Neither a lofty degree of intelligence nor imagination nor both together go to the making of genius.*
> *Love, love, love,*
> *that is the soul of genius.*
>
> Mozart

"It has been shown... that when there are two harps tuned to the same frequency in a room, one a large harp and the other smaller, if a chord is struck in the bigger harp it fills and infuses the little harp with the grandeur and beauty of its resonance and brings it into tuneful harmony. Then, the little harp sounds out its own tune in its own voice."

O'Donohue points out that, "This is one of the unnoticed ways in which a child learns to become herself. Perhaps the most powerful way parents rear children is through *the quality of their presence* and the atmosphere that pertains in the in-between times of each day. Unconsciously, the child absorbs this and hopefully parents send out enough tuneful spirit for the child to come into harmony with her own voice."

Whether you want to be or not, you are the big harp. The music you play will influence every other harp in the room.

Boom out discordant music and you will create discord in every other "instrument." Learn to play with power and harmony and you will bring forth the finest music from every "harp."

When is it difficult to be your best self? I slip out of mine when I am tired or have been unable to deflate my stress or feel caught up with someone's nitpicking. When this happens I default to irritability.

How can you be your own best companion? A true picture sketches *all* strengths and weaknesses.

None of us are saints. Paintings of saints routinely show them wreathed in light and crowned with halos. For centuries crowns have signaled power. The goal was to suggest that kings, queens or emperors were deities and should be treated as such. Although most power has moved away from hereditary leaders the gold, diamonds, tiaras and rich robes remain symbols or leadership in countries like Great Britain. Thus, the risk that leaders will think of themselves as gods remains.

This issue extends insidiously into hospitals where the "scepter" of power is the physician's stethoscope and the CEO's business attire. In a setting where clothing signals power a person wearing a patient gown is at risk for discrimination.

Leadership must come from intrinsic strength not superficial symbolism. What did Gandhi wear? What did Jesus wear? What do patient's wear? Are we granting patients the respect they need? Ultimately, light shines through every great leader. And it lives within you. How else explain why some seem transformed from ordinary beings to masterpieces of energy and power?

None of the great became so by reading a list of characteristics and adopting them. But all of them studied the lives of the famous. They read stories and from those stories shaped their own.

That is why *The Seven Powers of Radical Loving Leaders* is a storybook, not a textbook. Thousands of books have been written about the seven heroes profiled here. What may be new here is the application of the skills of great leaders from other areas to healthcare.

SUPERHEROES

Your being vibrates at this moment. Where is the light that can make your spirit sing? The vibrations in seven kinds of energy unlock your highest powers.

When I was a kid my friends and I argued about which superhero had the coolest powers. Was it Spiderman with his web–spinning talent? Was it Batman and his Batcar or, was it Superman, who could do everything, so long as there was no Kryptonite around.

Little kids are not inspired by old men like Churchill or slightly built stars like Mahatma Gandhi. It is the characters that can fly or score touchdowns or catch bullets that fascinate.

My youngest grandson pasted a sticker on the back of my cellphone. It is an image of the great and powerful "Spiderman."

Kids (especially little boys?) long to be big and powerful like the adults that tower over them. When they discover superheroes that are even stronger than their parents they bond with them.

One Sunday School teacher captures the attention of her seven-year-olds by talking about Jesus in superpower terms. Next to Jesus, Superman looks weak. Superman and Batman cannot heal the sick.

How many of us are still fascinated by superheroes; to have superpowers?

Good news! You already have them. And these powers can accomplish more than Superman.

Your smile will raise the energy of the next person you see. Your affirmation changes the blood chemistry of the people you compliment. Your willingness to listen and be present to others can heal their soul better than can Superman's x-ray vision.

"Want to change the world?" Mother Teresa asked. "Go home and love your family... We can do no great things. We can only do small things with great love."

Want to change the life of the patients and staff you work with? Go out and love them.

Every time I look at that Spiderman sticker on my phone I smile. It was placed there by one of my superheroes, a little grandson who has the power to make my heart leap tall buildings at a single bound.

> *We can only do small things with great love*
>
> Mother Teresa

YOUR DINNERS WITH THE GREATS

If you could invite one legend to dinner who would it be? Imagine each radical loving leader offering you an evening with them. Your host at each of seven dinners is a person who, despite being a regular human being, has changed the world.

Each legendary leader possessed every one of the seven powers and can be your teacher during your dinner and beyond. At the table, each will share with you one of his or her powers.

Listen to her or him and they will tell you the secret of their magic. When you leave you are free to use everything they teach you. You do not have to change millions like they did. All you have to do is use their powers to change yourself and the lives of those you lead.

Victor Frankl will show you how he marshaled his personal sense of meaning to survive a Nazi concentration camp. Look at how he taught the world a lesson that you can weave into your own heart.

Martin Luther King, a man unequipped with Superhero x-ray vision, applied leadership leverage to transform America. You can use that leverage in your life.

Reflect on how Mahatma Gandhi, a wisp of a man with a tiny voice, freed a nation of hundreds of millions from British rule. Can you free yourself from imprisoning life patterns?

Another wisp of a person gathered a group of thirteen nuns together and grew her ministry into a crowd of four thousand women who ministered to the poor. Mother Teresa did not battle criminals. She saved lives, as do you.

In 1940, before America entered the greatest war in history, all of Europe had fallen to the Axis Powers. One radical loving leader, Winston Churchill, was able to energize his fellow citizens to accomplish a miracle. His persistence leveraged the potential of a small nation to defeat a giant one. Join him for dinner.

What superhero could grab hold of the two halves of a nation and knit them back together? Only Abraham Lincoln mustered such strength. Sit across the table and listen to him.

As if possessing Superhero potions each leader has spun magic by engaging seven human powers. But, this is not about spells or tricks. This is not magic.

Each power contains natural energy. Each energy leverages exponential change.

Consider the seven powers of *all* radical loving leaders. Enjoy your seven dinners.

Part Two

The Powers

You see things; and you say, 'Why?'

But I dream things that never were; and I say, "Why not?"

George Bernard Shaw

The First Power
HIGH PURPOSE

He who has a Why to live for can bear almost any How.

Friedrich Nietzsche

Why is high purpose important? Across the arc of history hundreds of millions of people have died (a high percentage of these just in the 20th Century) because of the evil-purpose leadership of men like Hitler and Stalin. Millions more suffer because of the low purpose leadership of countless tyrants and misdirected managers, whether they are running countries or striking fear in the hearts of caregivers in your hospital as team leaders.

World War II, the greatest drama in the history of the world, serves as the backdrop from which three of the seven great leaders of the 20th century grew, including the first; a person who defined the power of purpose.

Your first dinner with a radical loving leader begins with the following story.

What you get by achieving your goals is not as important as what you become by achieving your goals.

Henry David Thoreau

By the spring of 1941 he had established a successful practice in neurology and psychiatry at the Rothschild Hospital in Vienna. His colleagues revered him.

He was also in love. In December he married Tilly Grosser. His love of her would save his life.

A rap on the door shattered Dr. Victor Frankl's beautiful life. It was September 25, 1942. The Nazis had come. Frankl and his wife were cattle-trained off to the Theresienstadt Concentration Camp. Surviving by his wits, will, and training, Frankl delivered radical loving care to other prisoners as best he could.

On October 19, 1944 an even worse disaster struck. Victor and Tilly were torn away from each other, dragged on board separate cattle cars and transported to Auschwitz—the most notorious murder machine in the vast Nazi concentration camp system.

Inmates were literally stripped of everything, down to their own nakedness. Wedding rings were ripped or cut off their fingers. Photographs of loved ones were grabbed and stomped on. Scraps of paper that bore the essence of Frankl's hard-won research on his book were taken and burned.

Frankl and his fellow inmates were forced to don striped uniforms that marked them as less than human in Nazi eyes. Frankl's wrists were tattooed with numbers that replaced his name.

Like the rest, Frankl was made to live on five ounces of bread and a few sips of watery soup each day. Sleep was short and was constantly interrupted by ruthless guards. Shrill whistles awakened inmates into hellish work conditions.

Frankl was awakened one night by a fellow inmate screaming amid a nightmare. Frankl started to awaken him. Then he realized that he would leave the man alone because how could the man's nightmare be worse than the one he would wake up to?

Men were compelled to sleep nine at a time in racks meant for two or three. Thus they literally slept with their bodies against each other.

Here, you could say, "I feel so sorry for them," or you can seek to empathize with this level of suffering by identifying it with your own moments of pain. Thus, Frankl's words may pierce your soul and lead you to a new understanding of purpose.

Struggling along an icy path one night Frankl felt cold, exhausted and hungry. Brutalized by guards and the winter he felt something worse than hunger, the loss of hope. Then, "as the stars were fading and the pink light of the morning was beginning to spread behind a dark bank of clouds," he experienced an epiphany.

In his landmark book, *Man's Search for Meaning*, Frankl suggests the brutality of his experience in one gripping page. If you want to capture a sense of the power of purpose read every word.

"We stumbled on in the darkness, over big stones and through large puddles, along the one road leading from the camp. The accompanying guards kept shouting at us and driving us with the butts of their rifles. Anyone with very sore feet supported himself on his neighbor's arm. Hardly a word was spoken; the icy wind did not encourage talk.

"Hiding his mouth behind his upturned collar, the man marching next to me whispered suddenly: "If our wives could see us now! I do hope they are better off in their camps and don't know what is happening to us."

"That brought thoughts of my own wife to mind. And as we stumbled on for miles, slipping on icy spots, supporting each other time and again, dragging one another up and onward, nothing was said, but we both knew: each of us was thinking of his wife.

"Occasionally I looked at the sky, where the stars were fading and the pink light of the morning was beginning to spread behind a dark bank of clouds. But my mind clung to my wife's image, imagining it with an uncanny acuteness. I heard her answering me, saw her smile, her frank and encouraging look. Real or not, her look was then more luminous than the sun that was beginning to rise.

> *...love is the ultimate and highest goal to which man can aspire.*
>
> Victor Frankl

"A thought transfixed me: for the first time in my life I saw the truth as it is set into song by so many poets, proclaimed as the final wisdom by so many thinkers. The truth that *love* is the ultimate and the highest goal to which Man can aspire.

"Then I grasped the meaning of the greatest secret that human poetry and human thought and belief have to impart: *The salvation of Man is through love and in love.* I understood how a man who has nothing left in this world still may know bliss, be it only for a brief moment, in the contemplation of his beloved.

"...For the first time in my life I was able to understand the meaning of the words, 'The angels are lost in perpetual contemplation of an infinite glory.'"

Frankl found even more reason to survive beyond his beloved. He developed a life-saving obsession to tell his story and to advance his theory that purpose was the defining power of life. Meaning gives hope. Purpose focuses our energy more effectively than any other force.

Man's Search for Meaning engages the most important journey of the Twentieth Century. It was written against the backdrop of six years in history, 1939-1945, when the entire world was engulfed in the horrors of World War II.

Frankl survived the war. Hitler, the man who started it, the evil dictator who spawned the concentration camps where Frankl suffered, did not.

World War II, because of its grand scale, includes every deep experience. Its stories teach you about your life and how to deal with patients who have been marginalized by broken systems.

A horror story told by a single man started World War II. Hitler's storytelling was so powerful that he convinced millions of otherwise civilized people that Jews were no better than rats. As people, Jews would have needed to live. As "rats" Nazis could exterminate them.

Hitler told a story that enchanted Germans beaten down by economic depression. He gave them purpose and hope grounded in hatred and fear. And from that a country of seventy million found the energy to terrorize the entire world.

The whole story would be ridiculous, except that so many millions believed it and acted on it. And they came stunningly close to success.

The Allies, led by Winston Churchill and Franklin Roosevelt, advanced a different and ultimately more powerful story, that democracy nurtured human life while fascism demeaned it. The Allies were good and Hitler was bad. Therefore we, the good guys, must win.

Amid this tragedy Victor Frankl was one of millions of "rats" that lay suffering in a Nazi concentration camp. He taught us the single most powerful life lesson that can change *your* life. He summarized the power of *meaning* by quoting Frederick Nietzsche: "He who has a Why to live for can bear almost any How."

Frankl saw the power of "why" in Auschwitz and Dachau. Emaciated prisoners often died within 24 hours of saying three words: "I give up."

Other equally weakened prisoners survived on a different three words: "I will live." That purpose and hope gave them an almost superhuman power to prevail.

People say, "Where there's a will there's a way." But without a "why" we become robots, or we may give up all together. Purpose drives energy.

Look at the story of one woman who was born into poverty, raped at age nine and a mother at fourteen of a baby who died in infancy. She sometimes had to wear dresses made of potato sacks. Ridiculed on the school bus for her poverty she stole to get money for better clothes.

All along, she nurtured her sense of purpose. She told herself one day she would be something.

One of her pastimes as a child was to interview her corncob doll and rows of crows. Not much future in that.

Her name is Oprah Winfrey.

Offering loving care to those in need is as fine a purpose as there is. This is a vision for change that offers hope because it values and validates everyday work.

But most hospitals dilute love's energy by fostering mission fraud instead of loving care. They post grand mission statements with lofty purposes but do not practice them. This leaves it to individual caregivers and some enlightened managers to nurture radical loving care. They cannot do it alone. They need complete support from top leadership. If the only people who care about mission are the mission director and a handful of idealistic employees *then loving care will slip to the bottom of the agenda.* Average performance will be tolerated and patients will be the victims.

Develop a high purpose. Shape it into a clear and inspiring vision. Change your world and that of those you lead. Do it for them and for the patients who trust you. Do it for yourself.

HIGH PURPOSE AND LOW PURPOSE ENERGY

Our low purpose instincts are always at war with our passion to engage high purpose energy. Baseball star Ty Cobb put up great numbers and some consider him a legend. But, his desire for success flattened his sense of high purpose. No one admires Cobb's reputation for dirty play and his bigoted racial views.

After consecutive victories in the Tour de France cycling star Lance Armstrong became one of the most admired athletes in history. When it turned out he had broken the rules and then lied repeatedly, his legacy was destroyed.

Since each of these individuals knew what was right how did they slip off course? Each claimed high purpose views. But, low-purposed desire for victory at any cost ended up costing them everything.

Because Jackie Robinson was a high-purpose leader he will live into history as a true success. His entry into baseball as the first black major-leaguer was a radical step. His passion for the game together with his talents and hard work endure as an illustration of radical loving leadership by example.

LOVE AND PARTNERSHIP AMONG SOLDIERS

Some people, typically men, worry about my use of the "love" word. Their concern is eased when they remember the words of soldiers in battle.

A television news report on troops returning from Afghanistan featured some illuminating interviews on love in wartime. Some soldiers had seen companions blown apart by roadside bombs. Others had felt limbs torn away and eyesight stolen forever. Many wanted to return with their platoons. "I love my guys," a burly sergeant said. "I'd do anything for them."

"I miss the companionship," a marine commented. That marine had missed his battle pals so much that, after a few months home, he returned to the front.

The reporter had continued to follow him. When the marine returned he was missing a leg. "This may sound stupid," he said. "But, I miss my buddies because I love them. I gave my leg for that and I don't regret it."

These people, like countless others around the world, had found purpose in their lives. They had found love.

Since love is the greatest power on earth, why not use it? Why not speak it?

Dr. Victor Frankl, the first Radical Loving Leader, was one of the millions that Hitler, a radical hating leader, sought to exterminate. Dr. Victor Frankl, the modern day author of meaning. Dr. Victor Frankl, who found purpose in a place Hitler designed to kill him, outlived Hitler by 52 years, 5 months and three days.

The Second Power
PASSION

Live your beliefs and you can turn the world around.

Henry David Thoreau

His father whipped him regularly until he was fifteen, telling a friend "he would make something of him even if he had to beat him to death." A nearly life-long sufferer of depression, the whipped boy jumped out of the second floor window of his Atlanta home at age twelve because he felt responsible for his grandmother's death.

From such hard beginnings, the whipped boy rose to become one of the most passionate and iconic leaders in the world. His legacy of radical loving leadership shines its light into your life today.

Passion can be satisfied, desire cannot. Passion produces peak performance. Desire is driven by anxiety and fear.

Passion must have a voice. And Martin Luther King, the man who was whipped as a boy, and ridiculed as an adult used his passion to fuel the most important American protest movement of the twentieth century.

Another legacy demonstrates passion gone wrong. Ten years before King's birth the man who would be an anti-hero to King was born in Alabama.

Segregationist Alabama Governor George Wallace was not a devil. His opponent, Martin Luther King, Jr. was not a saint. Yet, in spite of moderating his views later in life, Wallace will always be remembered as a bad leader who supported injustice. King will always be remembered as one of the greatest leaders in American history.

Wallace had a desire to be Governor, not a high purpose passion to serve. When he lost the 1958 nomination for governor to Ku Klux Klan supporter John Patterson he sold out any loving path he may have considered.

Wallace's comment following his first defeat is a jarring declaration of why he could never be a true success: "Seymore," he told his aide, "you know why I lost that governor's race? ... I was outniggered by John Patterson. And I'll tell you here and now, I will never be outniggered again."

When Wallace became governor it also became his fate to come up against an icon. The high-purpose passion of Martin Luther King, Jr., a man despised by millions of mid-twentieth century southerners, would end up exposing the darkness of Wallace's wrong-headed views.

How did King do it? Watch him on film. His passion burns hot as a bonfire and shines bright as the northern star.

But it took much more than speeches to change the centuries old institution of segregation. King's passion for his cause rose to genius level, motivating others to organize, to engage in non-violent protest and to march on through setback after setback.

THE STORY HEARD ROUND THE WORLD

At 6 pm on December 1, 1955 she did what she had done so many times before. She boarded the Cleveland Avenue bus after a full day of hard work. As she had done so many times before, she paid her fare. As she had done so many times before, she took her seat in the section marked "Colored Only."

At each stop, more whites boarded. Finally, the driver, James Blake, stopped the bus and moved the "colored only" sign a couple rows back to accommodate white riders. Blake told the four blacks in those seats, "Y'all better make it light on yourselves and let me have those seats."

Three rose and moved. On that winter day in 1955, Rosa Parks did something she had never done before. She stayed put. She was now sitting in the "Whites Only" section of the Cleveland Avenue bus.

Blake called the police. Parks was arrested and jailed. Her offense: riding in the white section of a segregated bus. The Montgomery bus boycott was born. It is a story of how a small number of regular people, led by a passionate man, transformed our nation.

Listen to what Parks would later write: "People always say that I didn't give up my seat because I was tired, but that isn't true. I was not tired physically, or no more tired than I usually was at the end of a working day. I was not old, although some people have an image of me as being old then. I was forty-two. No, the only tired I was, was tired of giving in."

> The soft-minded man always fears change.
> He feels security in the status quo, and he has an almost morbid fear of the new. For him, the greatest pain is the pain of a new idea.
>
> Martin Luther King

Parks, "tired of giving in," looked to Martin Luther King to free her from humiliation. He looked to her to help. Some professional caregivers across the country, fed up with bad bosses every day, may feel the same way. Leaders owe them more. Go deeper into the story to see how the message of Montgomery can affect your life today.

Many have heard of the Montgomery bus boycott. Few recall how long it took for the Civil Rights movement to gain victory in that town. The passion of Martin Luther King kept hope, and the movement, alive. Hundreds of African Americans depended on the bus to reach their employment. They risked their livelihood and their safety by walking, carpooling or biking to work. Negative peer pressure blocked whites from helping.

As the months dragged on there was no progress against stubborn officials. Protesters began to tire. Many black leaders began to favor compromise. They urged King to take baby steps instead of giant strides. A less passionate leader might have weakened. A more fragile heart might have been willing to move by inches instead of miles.

King stood strong.

Finally, after 381 days of struggle and suffering, the city yielded.

Are symbols important in leadership? The Cleveland Avenue bus in which Parks refused to move on that fateful December day is now enshrined in the Henry Ford Museum, in Detroit, Michigan. A full-size replica is housed in the National Civil Rights Museum in Memphis, Tennessee.

In Abraham Lincoln's first inaugural address he appealed to "the better angels of our nature. One hundred and one years later Governor Wallace, in his inaugural address, used words that forever mark him as a man of low purpose and failed vision: "I say segregation now, segregation tomorrow, segregation forever."

Months later, Wallace added more poison to his legacy by standing at the entrance of the University of Alabama to block black students from entry. I remember the television coverage. He looked ridiculous. The image of him in that doorway is a high example of low purpose leadership.

Love lived at the root of the Civil Rights cause and King's leadership. But the vast majority of Americans had turned a blind eye to southern discrimination for decades. This indifference included many northerners who classified segregation as a southern problem and none of their business.

> *. . .the only tired*
> *I was, was tired of*
> *giving in.*
>
> Rosa Parks

"TOUGH-MINDED AND TENDER-HEARTED"

We owe to Martin Luther King one of the finest leadership phrases ever spoken: "It is pretty difficult to imagine a single person having, simultaneously the characteristics of the serpent and the dove, but... We must *combine* the toughness of the serpent and the softness of the dove, *a tough mind and a tender heart.*" (emphasis added.)

Love defined King's strategy. He knew that his main audience was not southern governors but American voters. Violence might have lost those voters. Your audience is not always the person before you but others who are listening.

The use of non-violence, pioneered in part by Gandhi and as old as the teaching of Jesus lent a level of integrity to the cause that paid dividends. Bigots played into the hands of the movement when they bombed churches, turned fire hoses on protesters and beat demonstrators.

Ugly hatred was the face of the segregationist cause. Civil Rights demonstrators were robed in determination and crowned with grace. Tens of thousands of marchers got better results with peaceful protest than if they had armed themselves with guns.

Martin Luther King's passionate example wove golden threads into the fabric of the entire Civil Rights movement. He shaped a culture of victory by attracting followers who found their passion by watching his.

King's willingness to enter the front lines rather than to retreat to an office inspired others, as did his submission to imprisonment at a Birmingham jail and numerous other acts of courage. Throughout the struggle, King's passion inspired the weary and the disenfranchised. His leadership energy was contagious. Doubters, pessimists, traditionalists, laggards and even moderates are always a threat to significant causes. King faced down all of these negative energies and prevailed.

By the time Martin Luther King, Jr. rose to deliver his "I Have A Dream" speech it was easy for him to draw a crowd of hundreds of thousands and to command the attention of tens of millions through television and radio. Most national leaders lacked the courage to change. Southern senators and congressman had successfully blocked progress time after time. King's passionate leadership changed both the culture of his followers and the hearts of Americans. The passage of the Civil Rights Act in 1964 became a forgone conclusion.

On March 7, 1965 peaceful protesters crossed The Edmund Pettis Bridge into Selma, Alabama. Stuck on enforcing evil statutes in brutal ways the local police used a favorite tool of fear: They attacked the marchers with clubs and attack dogs. The images of bleeding protesters galvanized Washington leading to the passage of the 1965 Voting Rights Act.

The movement that changed our country for the better would not have happened *in the way that it did* without King and his radical passion.

Other leaders carrying different torches tried to incinerate King's message of love.

Four years before Martin Luther King's birth a baby named Malcolm Little was born. His father was killed when he was six and his mother was placed in a mental institution when he was thirteen. As Little grew to adulthood as a black man in America he became radicalized in a different way.

> *A nation that continues year after year to spend more money on military defense than on programs of social uplift is approaching spiritual death.*
>
> Martin Luther King

He was not always wrong. But he was always filled with "righteous" anger.

He called Martin Luther King, Jr. a "chump" and his followers "stooges of the white establishment." Against Martin Luther King's message of non-violence the man we know as Malcolm X wrote: "I am for violence if non-violence means we continue postponing a solution to the American black man's problem just to avoid violence."

He said, "I don't even call it violence when it's in self-defense; I call it intelligence." And finally, in a clever turn of phrase, Malcolm X said in the early 1960s, "Be peaceful, be courteous, obey the law, respect everyone; but if someone puts his hand on you, send him to the cemetery."

What if Malcolm X had been the dominant voice of the Civil Rights movement? Would protesters have been an army of the armed promoting killing and black segregation instead of a legion of love promoting integration? That is the difference the voice of Martin Luther King made, the leadership of love over the tactics of fear.

Many have forgotten that King took on another cause towards the end of his life. Once again it was controversial. Once again he was assaulted with calumny. Once again he was right. And once again he was ahead of his time.

On April 4, 1967, exactly one year before his assassination, Martin Luther King announced his opposition to the Vietnam War: "A nation that continues year after year to spend more money on military defense than on programs of social uplift is approaching spiritual death."

As King spoke these words Americans fought and died needlessly in a failed war. Some were pilots who were shot down in the skies above the rice paddies and imprisoned in horrifying prisoner of war camps. One of these tortured prisoners was my first cousin, Harlan Chapman, shot down November 5, 1965. Had the country, including President Lyndon Johnson, listened to King and brokered a peace my cousin would have been released and the lives of hundreds of thousands of soldiers and civilians would have been saved.

The war was a tragic mistake. But, millions who had backed Civil Rights marches could not see this truth and turned on King. The media blasted him. "*The Washington Post* declared that King had "diminished his usefulness to his cause, his country, his people."

But King saw a connection between The Civil Rights movement and the Viet Nam War: "We have been repeatedly faced with the cruel irony of watching Negro and white boys on TV screens as they kill and die together for a nation that has been unable to seat them in the same schools."

By the time public opinion shifted another year had passed and Martin Luther King was dead at age thirty-nine. My cousin and the rest of America's POWs were not released until February 12, 1973. Our country finally evacuated Viet Nam in defeat on April 30, 1975; eight years after King had called for peace.

Today, King is lauded for his radical loving leadership in another venue in addition to civil rights: For opposing a war.

In 1957, millions disagreed with King's approach on civil rights. In 1967, millions attacked King's stand on Viet Nam. Today, hundreds of millions know he was right on both counts. The government that once resisted his pleas now honors his birthday as a national holiday because Martin Luther King, Jr. was one of the greatest leaders in American history.

On April 16, 1963 the imprisoned Martin Luther King, Jr. wrote a message. His *Letter from a Birmingham Jail* includes one of the most memorable declarations in American history: "Injustice anywhere is a threat to justice everywhere."

How can we adapt such language to the world of healthcare? Cruelty to patients anywhere is a threat to kindness everywhere. The same is true in leader-to- leader encounters. Fear-based leadership has no place in radical loving leadership.

Where attention goes, energy flows. Great leaders focus their passion like a laser. As a result, energy flows in exponential ways towards the goals they choose, and the goals you choose. True success is impossible unless goals are tied to love.

> *Never doubt that a small group of thoughtful, committed citizens can change the world; indeed, it's the only thing that ever has.*
>
> Margaret Mead

Real change requires passion. But how do leaders like you and me develop it? Opposite examples appeared one afternoon when I interviewed two veteran obstetricians. They were partners in practice but not in views about their professions.

One doctor said, "I practice as an ob-gyn because I'm good at it not because I love it." The other doctor told me, "I love delivering babies. I

95

love coming into the delivery room, the whole feel of the place, holding the baby. It's such a privilege!"

The doctor who sought success by doing something only because he was good at it never achieved satisfaction. He ended up in a failed attempt to unionize doctors and subsequently retired.

The doctor who loved his work also loved his life. He was not a radical but his successful career illustrates the stark difference between desire and passion.

A good baseball player may *desire* home runs, but he or she will never be truly great unless he or she has a *passion* for the game.

A SMALL STAGE EXPERIENCE

It was a typically sunny Saturday in the backyard of our California home. Seven years old, I was running around our backyard excited about something I do not even recall. When I stopped to take a breath, my dad spoke words that

> *If you aren't fired with enthusiasm, you will be fired with enthusiasm.*
>
> Coach Vince Lombardi

caught in my heart. "Chip, I hope you never lose your enthusiasm."

At seven, it never occurred to me that enthusiasm was something you could "lose," something that might slip out of your pocket and slide down the drain. My dad was right, of course. Many times since then I have tumbled into valleys where dismay shoved enthusiasm into the shadows. Fortunately, it always returned.

"The successful [person] has enthusiasm," President Harry Truman wrote. "Good work is never done in cold blood; heat is needed to forge anything. Every great achievement is the story of a flaming heart."

Imagine trying to energize the Civil Rights movement of the 1950s and '60s with a tepid commitment. Imagine trying to develop Apple Computer with a leader who just liked the idea rather than was passionate about it.

A casual commitment won't cut it.

Great caregiving calls for radical love.

Yet, most CEOs feel stuck in crossfire. On one side are physicians in need of placation. On another are employees with demands.

On a third side is the community of patients, family and citizens with high expectations. On the fourth side is the group that draws the CEO's main attention—board members who are his employers. Most boards, particularly of non-profit organizations are populated with status quo thinkers. "The boat is sailing okay," one CEO told me. "I don't want to rock it."

If you want meaningful change embrace *a passion for transformation.* Otherwise you will find yourself reacting to the latest demands of multiple groups rather than pursuing a vision of excellence.

Passion lifted a couple of brothers in Minnesota out of obscurity to found the now world famous Mayo Clinic. Passion's energy drove an impoverished painter named Vincent Van Gogh to create art that adorns the walls of the greatest museums. Passion surged through the mind of Thomas Edison and into the light bulbs that illuminate our world.

Meaningful change requires fire for transformation.

Passion requires light to show the way.

The Third Power

POTENTIAL

The world is a possibility if only you'll discover it.

Ralph Ellison

On August 9, 1921 a tall, robust, thirty-nine-year-old fell off his boat and into the freezing cold Bay of Fundy. He laughed at his clumsiness. A fine swimmer, he quickly found safety.

The next day, he went sailing again, this time with his children. Afterwards, he jogged across the island he loved. It was the last time he would ever run.

Less than twenty four hours later, he could not move his legs. The next day, he was paralyzed from the chest down. By August 13 his shoulders and arms had weakened.

Even though movement returned above his waist he was condemned to a life of permanent paralysis. Polio had crippled his body but not his passion to serve.

Not until we are lost do we begin to understand ourselves.

Henry David Thoreau

Nine years later Franklin Roosevelt was President of the United States.

Roosevelt was re-elected three more times (the most a President will ever accomplish.) He led our country through its worst depression and captained our nation through the greatest war in history.

In September of 1921, no one (except perhaps Roosevelt himself) could imagine that the paralyzed man had the potential to become one of the finest Presidents in history. He would more likely live the cloistered life of an invalid.

Strapped into his leg braces, Roosevelt mined every ounce of his strength to run for office. Often confined to his wheelchair he mustered every gram of his potential to become a world-changing leader. What kind of attitude does it take to pursue what seemed an impossible dream? Roosevelt quipped "If you had spent two years in bed trying to wiggle your toe, after that anything would seem easy."

When FDR finally won the Democratic nomination for President in 1932 he had another obstacle. How would a rich man like him connect with the Depression-ravaged poor people whose vote he needed? The answer came a dozen years later from an industrial worker quoted by author Susan Ware: "Mr. Roosevelt is the only man we ever had in the White House who would understand that my boss is a son of a bitch," the worker said.

As President, the physically crippled FDR performed like an Olympic champion during his first hundred days in office. He launched his "New Deal" and birthed an economic recovery that brought a rapid rebound from 1933-1937. He immediately attacked the panic of The Depression by declaring, "The only thing we have to fear is fear itself." Most powerful of all, Roosevelt's leadership awakened the potential of the nation itself, inspiring millions to find the confidence to dig down and develop more of their gifts.

In 1941, it was not clear that America was the strongest nation on earth. The greatest power looked like Germany. The United States had not yet awakened to its own potential. Roosevelt startled it into action.

Under the leadership of a man in a wheelchair the United States rose, for the first time, to become the undisputed leader of the free world. In a world that had been dominated by dictators, Roosevelt managed to maintain balance. "The quality of his being," Labor Secretary Frances Perkins said, "made him one with the people...made it possible for him to be a leader without ever being, or thinking of being, a dictator."

Imagine yourself into FDR's life for one day. Pick February 7, 1942. On that day the world was caught in the vice grip of histories greatest war. You awaken on that morning recognizing that, in many ways, the future of the earth depends on you and your leadership. You turn to rise from bed. You cannot, of course. You, the most powerful leader in the world, must call for help to take your crippled body to the bathroom.

How can you possibly think your way through this challenge? What potential do you have to sustain the energy and heart needed to inspire your country and the world to supreme action? So many of us would want to hide rather than to confront such a daunting challenge.

Thinking your way into FDR's world for a moment offers several insights. One is the awareness that high potential can be found in the unlikeliest of people. The second is that, in some ways, leading a group of ten people has its own complex challenges. The third is that as you leave Roosevelt and return to your own world you can envision new strength in your own life. In your encounter with Franklin Roosevelt he has suggested to you what it takes to lead in your world by learning from how he led in his.

> *We are afraid to care too much, for fear that the other person does not care at all.*

Eleanor Roosevelt was not just a great first lady, she was one of the great leaders in American history. She also faced an obstacle people of her time knew nothing about. She was confronted with a mother-in-law who must have been among the most son-controlling women in history. Suffice it to say that FDR's mother managed his checking account until she died — and this was during her son's Presidency. For Eleanor, the Mother Test was a challenge of will against her Mother-in-Law!

First Lady Eleanor Roosevelt was a radical loving leader in her own right. She was a courageous campaigner for Civil Rights when that was a dangerous thing to be. In 1946 President Truman appointed her as delegate to the newly created United Nations where she became the first chairperson of the United Nations Commission on Human Rights.

Like every loving leader her wisdom helps us as leaders to this day. "You gain strength, courage and confidence by every experience in which you really stop to look fear in the face," she wrote.

If you are feeling frustrated because your team seems crippled, what can you do to mine their potential, to weld them into a team that consistently passes The Mother Test?

History is replete with examples of breakthrough leaders who labored against extraordinary handicaps. We enjoy music through our ears. Yet, a man who was deaf composed what is arguably the greatest symphony of all time. Beethoven created his 9th Symphony (sung as Ode to Joy) and conducted its debut without being able to hear a single note. Blind, deaf and mute from age two, Helen Keller became one of our greatest Americans.

Some of the most remarkable examples of extracting extraordinary potential from the ordinary come from the world of business.

I like the story of the fellow who grew up in a housing complex for the poor. His football skills enabled him to escape to college. After graduation he got a job with Xerox. One day he started working at a coffee shop. How many millions of us look at a cup of coffee and imagine nothing more than its taste or how the caffeine will affect them? This fellow saw something else in that coffee cup. Today, tens of millions of us buy coffee from his stores, called Starbucks.

"Growing up I always felt like I was living on the other side of the tracks," Starbucks founder Howard Schultz says, "I knew the people on the other side had more resources, more money, happier families. And for some reason, I don't know why or how, I wanted to climb over that fence and achieve something beyond what people were saying was possible. I may have a suit and tie on now but I know where I'm from and I know what it's like."

Howard Shultz climbed over the fence with nothing. On the other side, he founded 16,000 coffee shops and his net worth is $2.3 billion dollars.

Sheldon Adelson grew up sleeping on the floor of a tenement house. His father was a ne'er-do-well cab driver. Today, he is worth nearly $30 billion dollars.

What is the potential in a blank piece of canvas? If you were Pablo Picasso you could turn a couple dollars of paint, a brush and an empty rectangle into a masterpiece that might today be worth over $170 million dollars.

Thirty-one years before FDR was elected his cousin Teddy overcame childhood illness and asthma to become President, and is often ranked with his cousin and three others as one of the top five Presidents in history.

If you ever gaze into the Grand Canyon or breathe the fresh air near Yosemite National Park or revel in the geysers of Yellowstone please thank Teddy Roosevelt. The kid with asthma is the one who presided over the creation of our national park system and thus protected millions of acres from commercial development.

But what kind of accomplishment matters far more than money or fame or power? A baby is born. Who will that baby become? When he was a child, few recognized the potential in a carpenter's son born in Nazareth two thousand years ago.

You are so much stronger than you think you are. You have so much more talent than you may now imagine. So does your team.

> *Two kinds of players who ain't worth a damn: one that never does what he's told and the other that does nothing* except *when he's told.*
>
> Pro football coach "Bum" Phillips

Do not be a leader who blames your team for failure or complains that your team has no potential. And be sure and follow Coach Phillips advice along the way. Pick the right team members.

Spot the potential in your staff. Put the right person in the right job and nurture the talents of all. Simultaneously, develop your entire team into a peak-performing group.

NOTICING WEAKNESSES AS WELL AS STRENGTHS

Clearly, the greatest performers in history do not have the potential to be great at everything. Leaders sometimes forget this, struggling to make a terrific front line nurse into a capable leader when she or he would be better at continuing to give direct patient care, or straining to make a soldier into a sniper when he or she would be a better medic.

How often have you watched a terrific teacher struggle as a principal? Leading is different from teaching. Leading is different from nursing. Leading requires a completely different skill set than brain surgery.

The same is true in sports. Basketball star Michael Jordan is an average golfer. But, he was a genius on the basketball court. Joe Montana is a so-so basketball player. But he was a genius on the football field. Bart Starr was a legendary football quarterback. But he was unsuccessful as a coach.

Every person, team and organization has potential. But in some, it is buried so deep that even high inspiration and expert skill training cannot awaken it.

It is difficult (but possible) to change the culture of a sub-performing employee group. A weak medical staff is even harder to change because most doctors are independent, not employed, and doctors are the only ones who can admit patients.

ORDINARY EXAMPLE

Success is the marriage of the right choice and the right passion. I love baseball but I do not have the potential to become a great player.

Babe Ruth captured this issue in a comment that can guide every leader: "The most important thing that a young athlete must do is to pick the right sport. Not one that they just like a little but one that they love. Because if they don't really love their sport they won't work as hard..."

The most important thing a young leader can do is be sure they were meant to lead. If you do not have the potential and do not love leading, find another role as soon as possible. Are you meant to lead? Do you love leading?

The legendary Mickey Mantle said that "to play ball was all I lived for... I couldn't wait to go to the ballpark. I hated it when we got rained out." Do you love leadership that much? If you don't, you can learn to.

The first hospital I ran had many peak performing employees but we lacked the potential to become a great medical center. The average nature of the medical staff blocked our path in a way I could not overcome. But, our employees *could* give great competent and compassionate care. And they did.

The two other large hospitals did have the potential for greatness and I loved leading them there. Within three years of practicing loving leadership both organizations were performing at peak levels and were national leaders in patient and employee satisfaction.

Most hospitals have enough good employees and good doctors. They provide the base to move from good to great.

Love provides the light that illuminates your caregiving leadership and calls you to perform at your highest potential. Mine your potential to lift your leadership from just a job to a transformational calling.

The good news is that history proves that the right leaders can transform ordinary teams into energized groups who accomplish miraculous things.

A relative handful of people developed the atom bomb. A comparatively tiny group landed a man on the moon. A handful of people in a laboratory developed penicillin and another group in another lab created a vaccine that defeated polio.

Your team has the potential to deliver radical loving care. Help them do it.

The Fourth Power
PERSISTENCE

You cannot fail if you resolutely determine that you will not

Abraham Lincoln

Seven months pregnant, she walked the floors with the grace of a princess in a palace. In fact, she lived in a real palace.

Since her baby was not due until late January she ignored the initial vibrations of birth. But the baby boy inside her insisted on being born that day, November 30, 1874.

As a child, the boy developed a lateral lisp (then described as a stutter.) Although many call him the greatest speaker of the twentieth century he never shook it off.

"My impediment is no hindrance," Winston Churchill quipped to one crowd of listeners.

A speech impediment was far from the greatest obstacle Churchill had to overcome during his persistence-driven journey across more than sixty years of leadership. Some of his losses were disastrous. His victories were profound.

> *Genius is one percent inspiration and ninety-nine percent perspiration.*
>
> Mark Twain

He is a legend. If you were actually at dinner with him in 1955 at Number 10 Downing Street or at Blenheim Palace, you would have to put up with lots of cigar smoke and brandy. It might

107

be worth enduring that. He has enormous amounts to teach about persistence in leadership.

SAVIOR OF WESTERN CIVILIZATION?

Churchill is revered primarily for his robust leadership in the early days of World War II. Some credit him with saving western democracy after England, by herself, emerged successful against the Nazi advance.

By the summer of 1940, Hitler's blitzkrieg through country after country had essentially defeated all of Europe. With the United States still standing in the wings, England was the solitary obstacle between Hitler and total domination.

How do you create a persistent and hopeful vision when you are leading a small country against overwhelming odds? As Adlai Stevenson would subsequently say about Churchill, "He mobilized the English language and sent it into battle."

What does persistence look like? One unforgettable image emerged through a widely distributed portrait of Churchill, chomping on his cigar, staring fierce as a bulldog into the camera lens.

Another example shines through the words of an American visitor at the time, "Everywhere I went in London people admired [Churchill's] energy, his courage, his singleness of purpose. *People said they didn't know what Britain would do without him*...He was simply the right man in the right job at the right time." (Emphasis added.)

As the Nazis rained bomb after bomb on London, Churchill had to persist against another force. This time it was within. A segment of the

British public lobbied Churchill for a peace deal with Hitler. How do you maneuver around your own countrymen when they stand in your way?

Churchill declined compromise, although privately he expressed his doubts. On June 12, 1940, he told a colleague, "You and I will be dead in three months' time."

What are the tone and the language of high eloquence? Along with Lincoln, Churchill delivered some of the most inspired prose in history.

What would you say to your country if you were charged with leading a beleaguered nation (or your own team should they be under threat?)

On May 13, 1940, the day after the sixty-five-year-old Churchill took office, citizens waited breathless to hear their new leader's words. "I have nothing to offer but blood, toil, tears and sweat," he said.

And thus, he began to inspire not only his fellow citizens but also the world with a vision that has rung down through the years. It is well worth your time to study the conclusion to Churchill's remarks. Notice how he frames his country's vision. Every leader needs to learn from the great master.

"...You ask, what is our policy? I will say: It is to wage war, by sea, land and air, with all our might and with all the strength that God can give us; to wage war against a monstrous tyranny, never surpassed in the dark and lamentable catalogue of human crime. That is our policy.

"You ask, what is our aim? I can answer in one word: victory; victory at all costs, victory in spite of all terror, victory, however long and hard the road may be; for without victory, there is no survival.

"...At this time I feel entitled to claim the aid of all, and I say, 'Come then, let us go forward together with our united strength.'"

Look how Churchill frames the stakes. Confront people with such a challenge and they will draw out strength they did not know they had in order to prevail, especially if they are continually encouraged.

And continue to encourage Churchill did, using the power of repetition to phenomenal effect. Listen to these speeches on YouTube and read them now. Always remember that Churchill spoke these words on the brink of *the greatest conflict in the history of the world*:

"Even though large tracts of Europe and many old and famous States have fallen or may fall into the grip of the Gestapo and all the odious apparatus of Nazi rule, we shall not flag or fail."

Churchill faced off against Hitler with a certain *sangfroid*. It must have driven the Nazi leader mad to see images of Churchill flashing a Victory sign as he smiled at crowds of beleaguered Brits.

Note the energy he builds by repeating the language of defiance like a legendary sports coach.

"We shall go on to the end," Churchill said, "we shall fight in France, we shall fight on the seas and oceans, we shall fight with growing confidence and growing strength in the air, we shall defend our Island, whatever the cost may be, we shall fight on the beaches, we shall fight on the landing grounds, we shall fight in the fields and in the streets, we shall fight in the hills; we shall never surrender…"

Continuing this theme with his incomparable delivery, Churchill exhorted his nation in another legendary speech.

"…the Battle of Britain is about to begin. Upon this battle depends the survival of Christian civilization. Upon it depends our own British life, and the long continuity of our institutions and our Empire. The whole fury and might of the enemy must very soon be turned on us. Hitler knows that he will have to break us in this island or lose the war. If we can stand up to him, all Europe may be freed and the life of the world may move forward into broad, sunlit uplands.

Churchill framed his appeals with poetic language all the better to lift the hearts of his countrymen. All these years later, you can yet feel the tension that must have hung over the country and the world as he raised the stakes once again.

"…if we fail, then the whole world, including the United States, including all that we have known and cared for, will sink into the abyss of a new dark age made more sinister, and perhaps more protracted, by the lights of perverted science. Let us therefore brace ourselves to our duties, and so bear ourselves, that if the British Empire and its Commonwealth last for a thousand years, men will still say, *This* was their finest hour." (Emphasis added.)

So many coaches at halftime in the middle of a championship game have said to their team "This is it. Let this be your finest hour."

Finally, on August 20, 1940, after the small Royal Air Force had held off the Luftwaffe's first round of attacks, Churchill delivered what may be his most quoted speech—a classic of gratitude and appreciation:

"The gratitude of every home in our Island, in our Empire, and indeed throughout the world, except in the abodes of the guilty, goes out to the British airmen who, undaunted by odds, unwearied in their constant challenge and mortal danger, are turning the tide of the world war by their prowess and by their devotion. ***Never in the field of human conflict was so much owed by so many to so few.***" (emphasis added.)

The final phrase of this speech so inspired the people that it appeared on posters through the nation. It took more than a year longer, to December 7, 1941, before the United States finally joined England leading the Allies (including Russia) to victory.

Once again, I have heard this line quoted in hospitals to thank small groups for doing big things.

But, Churchill would owe even more to "the few." The worst lay ahead for England. Alone, they faced the terrifying Nazi "Blitz" from September 7, 1940 to May 21, 1941. Over those eight months, one week and two days, German bombs murdered more than 40,000 British citizens. (To put this in context, in March, 2015, 150 people were killed in the crash of a German plane in the French Alps. The number of British deaths in the Blitz is equivalent to 267 such deadly plane crashes!) In addition, more than one million homes were destroyed or damaged.

Churchill and his fellow citizens fought on. Suddenly, on May 22, 1941, the Luftwaffe vanished from the night skies of England. In the most colossal mistake of WW II, Hitler pivoted the might of the Nazi war machine east. There lay the land of his giant ally, the Soviet Union. He attacked them.

> *Our greatest weakness lies in giving up. The most certain way to succeed is always to try just one more time.*
>
> Thomas Edison

A month after Churchill's England won the Battle of Britain Hitler launched Operation Barbarossa against his own ally. Four million enemy soldiers that could have been used to defeat Great Britain were drawn into a Russian land that would chew up Hitler's army and swallow millions in a chasm of snow.

Winston Churchill, like Lincoln and Roosevelt and King, saved a way of life for us. Can we convert our gratitude to them into our own, high purpose crusades against suffering?

CHURCHILL'S EARLY HISTORY OF DEFEATS

The path the three great religions traveled began in the same place with the ancient teachings of the Old Testament. As King Solomon said in *Proverbs*, "...do no violence to the righteous; though they fall seven times they rise again." Persistence is the wisdom of the ages.

Churchill practiced that wisdom. He tried and failed as frequently as he succeeded on his way to immortality. He is a shining profile in persistence.

He was imprisoned in a POW camp during The Boer War. In 1899 he ran for Parliament and lost. Subsequently elected, his own constituency "deselected" him months later and he was compelled to run for office in another district. He lost.

As British Home Secretary in 1911 he insisted on being present at a police siege of a house occupied by Latvian anarchists. After the house went up in flames he stopped the fire brigade from dousing the inferno.

"I thought it better to let the house burn down rather than spend good British lives in rescuing those ferocious rascals," Churchill said, disgusting many Brits including Arthur Balfour who mocked him, "...he and a photographer were both risking valuable lives. I understand what the photographer was doing, but what was [Churchill] doing?"

In 1913 he made the terrible mistake of supporting sterilization of "the feeble-minded" versus institutionalization.

After backing the disastrous and bloody Gallipolis campaign in World War I he was forced out of his post as First Lord of the Admiralty.

In 1922, following an appendectomy, Churchill lost his Parliamentary seat again generating a classic Churchill quip: "I left without an office, without a seat, without a party and without an appendix."

A year later he ran again and lost again.

As Chancellor of the Exchequer in 1926 he made the horrific mistake of campaigning for Britain's return to the gold standard. This led to The General Strike of 1926.

After another series of miscues starting in 1929 and including his unfortunate and long term opposition to Indian independence, Churchill's political standing fell so far that he went into a self-imposed exile.

A decade passed before Churchill finally burst onto the world stage. His persistence won the day and saved Europe as well as the British Empire.

Imagine the difficulty of defeating Hitler if the United States and other Allies had not been able to stage attacks on the Axis powers (including the D-Day invasion) from posts in England. Consider the thousands, perhaps millions, of more lives that would have been lost if Churchill had not "marshaled the English language and sent it into battle."

THE HIGH PURPOSE LEADER
WHO TRIED TO KILL A DEVIL

Into 1944, Churchill and Roosevelt led the free world's purposeful effort to defeat the war machines of Germany and Japan. Hitler's Nazis continued to cause the deaths of millions in battle and millions more in concentration camps.

In total, the fatal decision by millions of Germans to heed Hitler's perverted mission statement and evil vision resulted in the deaths of *more than fifty million people* (on the Western Front of the war.)

While Churchill and Roosevelt sought to defeat Hitler with massive military assaults another man campaigned to accomplish the same goal with a single bomb. A courageous profile of high purpose opposition appeared in the last full year of the war. Claus Von Stauffenberg, a colonel in the German army, embraced another purpose. He decided he could save the

world by killing just one man, Adolf Hitler, the Devil personified.

At 12:35 p.m. on July 20, 1944 Von Stauffenberg entered a military briefing room and tilted his briefcase against a heavy oak table leg a few feet from where Hitler stood. The briefcase held a live time bomb.

At 12:38, the colonel left the room. At 12:42, the bomb exploded.

Photo: Von Stauffenberg on left.

Four were killed instantly. Impossibly, Hitler emerged from the wreckage like a Phoenix from the ashes. Squinting through the smoke, he thought, "I am fated to save the world." He then resolved to destroy it.

Barely thirteen hours later, a firing squad gathered on a field lit by truck headlights. They raised their rifles. Moments before his body was filled with bullets Claus Von Stauffenberg shouted his dying vision, "Long live our sacred Germany!"

To enhance your leadership learning consider again the impact of one being on the entire world. What does it mean that the high purpose life of Von Stauffenberg was lost and the evil-purpose power of Hitler continued?

How many lives turned on the failure of that bomb to kill the most murderous man in world history? The short answer is that millions more suffered and died because Adolf Hitler survived.

> *We took this challenge before our Lord and our conscience, and it must be done, because this man, Hitler, he is the ultimate evil.*
>
> Claus von Stauffenberg

The Allies under Churchill and Roosevelt were moving inland after the D-Day landing of June 7, 1944. Many thought the war was over. Most people failed to appreciate the significance of Hitler's homicidal mania.

Facing a lost cause, Hitler considered two brutal goals, "How can I throw more soldiers into battle and how many more Jews can I kill." It never occurred to him that it was time to save lives and end suffering by negotiating a peace. Some who suggested this humane notion were executed.

To sense the enormity of the tragic period between 12:42 pm July 20, 1944 and 2:41 am May 7, 1945 when Germany surrendered consider the deaths and killing in that hellish block of time.

Imagine the legions of your fellow caregivers who struggled to treat causalities arriving from those killing fields. Picture running a hospital in Berlin as bombs fell around you or a hospital in Britain flooded with more and more casualties every day and night. In the twenty-first century you can try to imagine your fellow leaders directing severely understaffed hospitals in Syria, or Afghanistan or Iraq amid war.

Forty-thousand men died at the Battle of the Bulge between December 16, 1944 and January 25, 1945. During the fall and winter of 1944 and the spring of 1945, a quarter of a million Jews died in camps and death marches ordered by Hitler's generals after the failed plot.

Because Hitler, although facing certain defeat, continued to refuse to surrender, more than a half million more soldiers and civilians died in battles around Berlin. By the time the Soviets captured the German capital, Hitler had finally done to himself what Van Stauffenberg had given his life to accomplish. On April 30, 1945, he hid in his bunker like a rat. With Russian soldiers closing in on him, Adolph Hitler committed suicide.

In all, there were well over five million deaths and other casualties after the failed plot to kill Hitler. In the fifteen tries to assassinate the Fuehrer Van Stauffenberg's effort came the closest to succeeding. His purpose could not have been nobler or clearer. His courageous leadership of dozens of conspirators nearly saved the lives and bodies of millions.

The spring and summer of 1945 was also an important year for three of the seven giants profiled in *The Seven Powers of Radical Loving Leaders*. On April 12, 1945, just eighteen days before Hitler's suicide, Franklin Roosevelt died. He would not see the end of the war through which he had led America so valiantly. Three days before Hitler's death, Dr. Victor Frankl was liberated from Dachau. One year later *Man's Search for Meaning* was published. On July 26, 1945 the incredibly popular Winston Churchill lost his re-election campaign. Typical of his persistence, he ran again five years later at the age of seventy-six, conquored his opponent, and served as British Prime Minister until he was eighty.

TWIN PROFILES OF PERSISTENCE

It took astonishing persistence to gain the right to vote for half of America's population. In 1848, the Seneca Falls Convention, the first women's rights convention, passed a resolution calling on Congress to let women vote. Even some of the organizers thought the request might be too radical.

In 1869, four years after the Civil War ended, two Radical Loving Leaders, Susan B. Anthony and Elizabeth Cady Stanton, founded a national organization supporting a woman's right to vote. They spent their lives advancing the cause.

Not until 1920, seventy-two years after the Seneca Falls Convention, did the United States finally allow women into the voting booth.

BLUNT WORDS AND GRUNT WORK

Examples of the power of stubbornness always characterize loving leadership. In one more illustration, senior officers in the early 1950s told Hyman Rickover he could not use a Navy base to build prototypes for his proposed nuclear submarine. Undaunted, he took his plans to private industry.

Predictions were that it would take twenty-five years to manufacture a nuclear sub that could stay submerged for months at a time. Rickover's sub was launched in four.

The blunt truth is that fine principles are not enough. Admiral Rickover, the founder of the nuclear navy, was frequently confounded by what he called the rarity of "talk-do" leaders. Politicians and even many top military leaders were great at talking big and acting small—or not acting at all.

COURAGE, LAUGHTER, AND A PERSONAL EXPERIENCE

Instead of being charged to assassinate an evil world leader or to develop a nuclear submarine all you have to do is remove a bad caregiver. Of course, that can be tough. That is why you are a leader.

As my son and I once discussed, it is courage and laughter that can save you on dark days. These two characteristics can unlock Love's magic.

I like Tennyson's language, "Come now, friends, 'tis not too late to seek a newer world... for my purpose holds/ To sail beyond the sunset/ and the baths/ Of all the western stars, until I die."

It is courage that enables you to sail on when your heart loses hope. Courage enables Love, faith and hope. Many hard experiences have taught you and me about persistence.

It was one of the worst days of my life. I remember early evening light falling through newborn leaves. I recall the way it pooled on the path I walked through the campus of Northwestern University on that day in the spring of 1963.

It was the last day I would live free of chronic illness. A few steps further down the path I felt a flaming poker burning within. A few days later, I was diagnosed with Crohn's Disease, an illness for which there is no cure.

At age nineteen, ambitious for success, I had been taking on challenge after challenge including running for student office while earning poor grades. I had also caught my girlfriend with another man, a particular trauma for a young romantic like me.

The three-way stress took its toll. My doctor told me I had five times the risk of developing cancer. Many teenage patients with similar diagnoses (like the young Dr. Rachel Remen) had been told they might not live to age forty.

Doctor Etheridge warned me against any kind of stressful career. When I described plans to become a lawyer he scoffed and said, "That could kill you."

Decades later, my biography reflects that the doctor's advice fell on deaf ears. But, there were many nights when I lay bleeding and in pain on bathroom floors when I thought Dr. Etheridge may have been right. Anyone who has suffered with a chronic illness knows the loneliness of acute agony and chronic suffering.

They know the worries of walking through a day struggling to conceal pain. They know what it is like to face the prospect of an early death.

Since age forty-six I have been hospitalized twice with life-threatening relapses. If you have walked on the burning coals of such a gamut you know the vital importance of Radical Loving Care.

When times are worst, logic tells you to give up and meaning fades. Beyond medicine, only raw persistence, faith and a dose of laughter can carry you through. At least it has for my son and me.

THE LIE ABOUT WINNING

It is a lie that winning is the only thing that matters.

The truth is opposite. Show me a good loser and I will show you a winner. Show me a bad winner and I will show you a loser. Clearly, we all need to succeed. Because success is about how it is achieved as well as whether it is accomplished, victory always comes to he or she that lives love.

When a physician friend died his obituary reported that, "He lost his battle with cancer." This odd (and frequent) observation suggests my friend was a loser. Life is not a football game.

If you die of old age can we say you lost your battle with death? If so, you and I will lose.

My friend was a caregiver. He did not "lose." His victory came from living love to life's end. If I die of cancer I hope no one says I "lost" my battle. I will not even have lost my life because I know I have tried—to the point of straining my potential.

Ralph Ellison wrote that the greatest affirmation of humanity is our willingness "to persist in the face of certain defeat." To face defeat and never retreat sounds foolish. But, to rest and return to trying expresses life.

This does not always need to be a grim endeavor. In fact, laughter (as Churchill and Lincoln proved repeatedly) can pave the way to victory.

When the San Francisco 49ers got the ball in the 1989 Superbowl the clock read 1:08 in the fourth quarter. The 49ers were five points behind and stuck on their own eight yard line. Eighty thousand fans screamed, hundreds of millions watched on television. As eleven members of the vaunted Cincinatti Bengals waited to tackle him the legendary Joe Montana stepped into the huddle to address his team. The 49ers were an impossibly long ninety-two yards from victory. Scoring in so little time from so far away seemed undoable. The Bengals were already imagining their own celebration.

Montana saw the tension on the faces of his teammates. Was there anything he could say that would ease that stress so that his team could perform at their best?

What would you say?

Here are the words Montana chose, "Hey guys, I just saw that John Candy is up in the stands. That guy is hilarious."

The players laughed. Humor opened their best energy. A minute later, they scored the winning touchdown.

THE HIGHEST MORAL IMPERATIVE

Our highest moral imperative is not to succeed but to always try. You have so much more courage than you think you do. Try even if you are tired. Try especially if you fail. Try even if you are frustrated from trying before. Nurture your strength. Help others try.

> *When you reach the end of your rope, tie a knot and hang on.*
>
> Abe Lincoln

You can only succeed if you try. You only fail when you give up, when you do nothing, when you ignore someone you could have helped, when you live never using your gifts because you were too fearful (or unmotivated) to try.

Persistence overcomes resistance. I would rather be a "has been" then a "never was."

Sing, Paint, Write, Lead, Love. Do all these things with artistic intent. Help the poor. Try things you are not good at as well as those things where you know you can succeed. If you persist you will always prevail, even if you fail to reach your goal.

Trying offers its own reward, that at the end of your days you can say that you strived, that you lived love to the last syllable of your life. In that way, you will, "sail beyond the sunset / and the baths / of all the western stars," until you die.

"BE THE BAT"

Coaches find different ways to train their players to perform in "the zone." I have heard coaches call out to baseball players, "Be the bat," or, in basketball, "Be the ball."

What the heck does this mean?

Many years ago I was watching a Boston Celtics game when the color announcer made an odd comment during a time out. It was the second quarter and the great Larry Bird had already scored twenty points.

"Watching Larry Bird reminds me of the pianist Arthur Rubenstein," the commentator said.

"What the hell does that mean?" the play-by-play announcer asked.

> *When you commit deeply your subconscious supports your consciousness.*

"Rubenstein was asleep and dreamed he was playing the first movement of the Rachmaninoff Second Piano Concerto when his phone rang," the color commenter said. "Rubenstein talked on the phone for ten minutes. When he hung up he discovered that he was into the second movement of the concerto. It had been playing subconsciously throughout the call."

"Okay," the play-by-play man said. "What does that have to do with Bird?

I will never forget the answer. "Larry Bird is *always* playing basketball. When he's eating breakfast that ball is bouncing along in his subconscious. When he is asleep he is shooting free throws. That is one reason he is so great."

The best surgeons commit to their art and thus engage both their subconscious and conscious energies.

Top leaders persist and commit in such a deep way that, at some level, their leadership story is always playing. They are always "playing basketball" or "playing the piano" or "leading." That is one way they overcome obstacles.

One way to put yourself into a position to lead is to learn what persistence looks like. You saw that in the story of Victor Frankl. Frankl reports that inmates often died within twenty-four hours of saying three words: "I give up." Frankl and other survivors, equally weakened physically, never said those words.

Margaret Mead wrote that you must "Never doubt that a small group of thoughtful committed citizens can change the world; indeed, it's the only thing that ever has."

Many great leaders and performers believe that *persistence is the single biggest key to success*. They know that if no obstacles are encountered then your vision is not bold enough and your challenge is not big enough. Those who turn back when barriers, both predictable and unpredictable, appear are guaranteed to fail.

Dr. Victor Frankl, Martin Luther King, Winston Churchill, Florence Nightingale, Bill Gates, Clara Barton, the Mayo Brothers and every other great leader, refused to give up in the face of ferocious obstacles.

You are never guaranteed success, but all great leaders persist.

Persist. Succeed as someone who, at least, has tried.

Winston Churchill admired the poem "If" written by his contemporary, Rudyard Kipling in 1885 as a letter to the poet's son. It was published in 1910.

It is the poem that begins with the well-known lines, "If you can keep your head when all about you / are losing theirs and blaming it on you..." and it ends with language that could well have been Churchill's life guide:

If you can talk with crowds and keep your virtue,
Or walk with kings—nor lose the common touch;
If neither foes nor loving friends can hurt you;
If all men count with you, but none too much;
If you can fill the unforgiving minute
With sixty seconds' worth of distance run,
Yours is the Earth and everything that's in it,
And—which is more—you'll be a Man my son!

The Fifth Power
POSITIVITY and HUMOR

On a February day two centuries ago a winter wind skirted barren trees searching for cracks to penetrate not a palace but a tiny home in the woods. Inside, a husband slid a candle towards his wife and lifted her groaning shoulders.

In spite of the cold, sweat silvered Nancy's brow as she made her final push. On February 12, 1809, amid candlelight, she delivered her baby boy into the only room in her house.

When her baby's life ended fifty-six years later some would compare the cabin of his birth to the stable where Jesus was born.

His life is so revered that you have carried his picture with you in your life. It is on the five-dollar bill.

Between birth and his victory in 1860, Abraham Lincoln was only elected to a federal office one time and served only one term as a congressman. Hatred of him in some corners was so homicidal that he arrived in Washington for his inauguration dressed in a disguise. The *Baltimore Sun* editorialized: "Had we any respect for Mr. Lincoln, official or personal, as a man, or as President-elect of the United States the final escapade by which he reached the capital would have utterly demolished it... We do not believe the Presidency can ever be more degraded by any of his successors than it has by him, even before his inauguration."

Hardly an auspicious beginning for the leader who remains a beacon of positive thinking to millions. Amid constant criticism and devastating loses on the battlefield Lincoln frequently suffered from what is now diagnosed as clinical depression. Yet, his belief in his country never waned.

Perhaps Lincoln's bouts of melancholy were triggered by his compassion for the deaths of so many hundreds of thousands of soldiers he sent into battle in the Civil War. No doubt it was aggravated by the deaths of two of his sons.

Halfway through the war, half his children dead, Lincoln said to an aide, "If there is a place worse than hell than I am in it."

Somehow, he conjured hope for his fellow citizens. And never once allowed himself the luxury of public negativity. Instead, his muscular language rallied our nation to a victory that reunited the sundered states. Throuth the arithmetic of power, this enabled America to become, in the 20th century, the world's leading nation.

"BETTER ANGELS"

As the dark clouds of war gathered Lincoln appealed to the best in people—offering hope in his first inaugural address: "The mystic chords of memory... will yet swell when again touched by the better angels of our nature."

A positive tone inspires a belief in success.

That is the kind of thing loving leaders do. They appeal to "the better angels of our nature." They stir the cauldron of human energy with their powerful presence and their sunlit words. Thus, alchemically, they brew a mixture that ignites the power of love in this world.

Great events can provide a platform for the potentially great to become the actually great. In the darkest days of the Civil War Lincoln's positive strength shined the brightest. Four and a half months after the Battle of Gettysburg, the remains of some of the fifty-thousand dead had still not been buried.

On November 19, 1863, within range of stacks of caskets, Lincoln rose to honor the memories of the Union soldiers who spent their last day on the bloodied ground. Less than three minutes later, he concluded his speech with this hope-drenched declaration:

"...we here highly resolve that these dead shall not have died in vain—that this nation, under God, shall have a new birth of freedom—and that government of the people, by the people, for the people, shall not perish from the earth."

Noted historian Gary Willis opined that "Abraham Lincoln transformed the ugly reality into something rich and strange—and he did it with 272 words. The power of words has rarely been given a more compelling demonstration."

The Civil War was the bloodiest in our history. A century and a half later its legacy remains rich for the families of many Americans.

Just six days after the Gettysburg Address a Confederate soldier fighting in the Battle of Armstrong Hill aimed his rifle at a Union soldier and fired. The lead ball struck my great grandfather, Private Harlan Chapman, in the right hip. Had it entered his body a few inches to the left neither I nor any of my Chapman relatives would be alive. He carried that bullet in his hip for the rest of his life.

Private Chapman, like millions of others, looked to President Lincoln for inspiration as well as strong and competent leadership. Lincoln provided it beyond the highest expectations of the times.

Lincoln was to be inaugurated for a second term March 4, 1865. Because of the miserable weather, the new Vice President Andrew Johnson took the oath in the musty Senate chamber. Senator Zachariah Chandler, an eyewitness, wrote that "the Vice President Elect was too drunk to perform his duties and disgraced himself and the Senate by making a drunken foolish speech."

The weather cleared enough for Lincoln to go outside for his inaugural address. Beneath the newly constructed Capitol Dome he addressed a crowd standing in thick mud. In his second inaugural address he articulated, in a single closing paragraph, as positive a vision as has ever been spoken by a President:

"With malice toward none, with charity for all, with firmness in the right as God gives us to see the right, let us strive on to finish the work we are in, to bind up the nation's wounds, to care for him who shall have borne the battle and for his widow and his orphan, to do all which may achieve and cherish a just and lasting peace among ourselves and with all nations."

Ted Widmer, assistant to the president of Brown University, wrote in *The New York Times* (March 3, 2015,) about the humble tone in the greatest inaugural speech in history, "Only once did [Lincoln] use the favorite word of politicians, 'I.'"

Photo: Booth is on the balcony just above and to the right of Lincoln.

So much of history's highest drama turns on the juxtaposition of great good and profound evil. Amid the crowd who heard Lincoln's declaration of "malice toward none" stood one listener poisoned with malice toward one. Pictures of the event show that John Wilkes Booth, Lincoln's assassin, was watching that day. In an enlargement of one photograph of the event Booth is visible standing on a balcony on a dozen feet above Lincoln. (Also, standing a few feet below Lincoln is co-conspirator Lewis Paine who failed in an attempt to kill Secretary of State William Seward.) Booth later told a friend, Samuel Knapp Chester, "what an excellent chance I had to kill the President, if I had wished, on inauguration-day! I was on the stand, as close to him nearly as I am to you."

Booth was present again on April 11, 1865 and heard the President utter words that may have sealed the death sentence of both Lincoln and his assassin. The President spoke of his plans to let African-Americans vote. Widner wrote, "That simple determination enraged [Booth], and precipitated the final act."

Four days later Abraham Lincoln sat in Ford's Theater enjoying the play "My American Cousin." Knowing victory was close he must have felt a canticle of thanks rising in his tired heart. The heart of John Wilkes Booth was flooded with the toxin of revenge. It was Good Friday. If only the sainted Lincoln had survived the bullet the way the devil Adolph Hitler would survive the bomb blast seventy-nine years later.

Before April reached its end, Booth himself lay dead in a burning barn in northern Virginia.

Instead of silencing the President's voice of hope, as Booth had sought to do, Lincoln's words and actions and the teachings he offers to you, survive to this day. But at the time, the Booth assassination led to the instant inauguration of the man who had been "too drunk to perform his duties" just six weeks before. Andrew Johnson's opposition to the Fourteenth Amendment, giving citizenship to African Americans (something Lincoln would clearly have supported) led to his impeachment by the House of Representatives. He was only acquitted in the Senate by one vote.

Thus, Booth's killing of our greatest President threw the country under the clumsy cudgel of one of our worst, Andrew Johnson.

The failure of high purpose by Confederate leadership, including their insistence on enslaving African Americans, resulted in a war which cost more than a million lives and untold suffering. If only the south had listened to Lincoln's radical loving leadership.

Time and again in hospitals and hospices I have seen too many Radical Loving Leaders retire (or be removed) only to be replaced by leaders whose most obvious traits are incompetence and/or lack of compassion. The leader makes a huge difference. Replace a good one with a bad one, or vice versa, and you will see that difference immediately.

A positive leader can turn around a poor performing team in a matter of months. A negative leader can take a fine team and drive it into the ground in weeks. The great problem is that most bad leaders do not realize they are strangling the finest flowers in the garden. Some good leaders lack the strength to weed out poor caregivers.

WORDS THAT MOVE NATIONS

Many leaders underestimate the power of words. If you study the morphology of the speeches of King, Roosevelt, Churchill and Lincoln you will be struck by the way they use language. Most great leaders have this gift. It is worth cultivating.

The conclusion of King's "I Have a Dream" speech rings in our hearts today. FDR spoke "The only thing we have to fear is fear itself." Churchill told his followers it was their "finest hour." Lincoln intoned "malice toward none and charity toward all."

These are the words that, spoken by Radical Loving Leaders, move nations. In a very small way, this is the kind of example I tried to follow when I asked leaders to take care of the people who take care of people.

A TRIO OF RADICAL LOVING LEADERS

Across the ocean, at the same time Lincoln was seeking to reunite our nation, another great leader applied high purpose with world changing results.

Millions of nurses still look to the example of a single woman, Florence Nightingale. It was Nightingale who laid the foundation for professional nursing at St. Thomas Hospital in London in 1860.

"The Lady with the Lamp" cast her light into nurse's lives and the lives of multitudes of the sick. She had no superpower ability to fly through the air. Her power was much greater than that.

During the American Civil War four years later a Confederate bullet tore through the sleeve of one of America's greatest leaders as she tended to a patient. She was unhurt, but her patient was killed.

She was Clara Barton, the pioneering woman referred to as "The Angel of the Battlefield." Years later, she founded The American Red Cross.

In the primitive medicine of the Civil War the frequent job of surgeons was to cut off arms and legs to save patients from gangrene.

Many times the amputations were unnecessary but loving care gave way to efficiency. When ether was in short supply, doctors sawed limbs off screaming men, then turned to a terrified line of waiting soldiers and shouted, "Next!"

Who brought some measure of compassion and fundamental order to that carnage? Dorothea Dix rose up to lead. She established and headed the nursing corps for the Union Army. Her dedication to caring for soldiers of both sides earned her criticism, resistance and enduring admiration. She resigned at war's end never having been paid a penny for her years of courageous work amid conditions today's caregivers could hardly imagine.

THE POSITIVE POWER OF WIT

He is a barbarian, Scythian, Yahoo, a gorilla in respect of outward polish, but a most sensible straight-forward old codger.

Lawyer George Templeton Strong on Lincoln.

Abraham Lincoln, the man with the chronic melancholy, also had a legendary sense of humor, a gift that informed others that the leader of their country was self-confident enough to jest. He knew that humor could disarm opponents.

Lincoln believed so strongly in the power of humor that he once preceded a meeting discussing the Emancipation Proclamation by telling a joke. When some of his cabinet members frowned, Mr. Lincoln said: "Gentlemen, why don't you laugh? With the fearful strain that is upon me night and day, if I did not laugh I should die, and you need this medicine as much as I do."

An anxious heart needs relief. A heavy heart needs rest from carrying so much weight. We all need humor especially amid the often-grim atmosphere where we minister to the sick and wounded.

Abe Lincoln could turn a phrase as well as anyone of his time. Adhere to his wisdom and enrich your leadership. "Elections belong to the people," he said. "It's their decision. If they decide to turn their back on the fire and burn their behinds, then they will just have to sit on their blisters."

Lincoln often used humor in the manner of judo or Tai-chi. In American boxing, you meet punch with punch. In Judo and Tai-chi you give with the punch, let it go by, and convert negative energy into positive.

"The best way to destroy an enemy is to make him a friend," Lincoln said.

So few leaders think like this. Instead, when someone swings at them, they swing back. Imagine defusing bad energy by converting negative to positive, by making a friend out of an enemy instead of trying to destroy him or her.

He used the same kind of thinking when he commented about an enemy, "I don't like that man. I must get to know him better." Gaunt-faced and roughened by the sun, no one ever accused Lincoln of being handsome. He turned this to his advantage. "After forty, every man gets the face he deserves," he told a group.

Once he was accused of being a two-faced liar. Using his appearance as a soft sword, he said, "If I were two-faced, would I be wearing this one?" In the same vein, he put everyone at ease when he said, "The Lord prefers common-looking people. That is why he makes so many of them."

"I am a firm believer in the people," Lincoln observed. "If given the truth, they can be depended upon to meet any national crisis. The great point is to bring them the real facts, and a beer." (President Obama, a student of Lincoln, tried the beer approach with Speaker of the House John Boehner. It worked with Boehner but did not transfer to Boehner's further right wing colleagues.)

How do you move someone who stubbornly insists on the wrong facts? Maybe Lincoln's lines will help: "How many legs does a dog have if you call the tail a leg?" Then he answered his own question: "Four. Calling a tail a leg doesn't make it a leg."

Feeling good about your success but wanting to sound humble? Here is what Lincoln said, "I'm a success today because I had a friend who believed in me and I didn't have the heart to let him down."

During the battles over slavery that provoked a Civil War an astonishing number of Americans claimed that enslaving people was good for them—that black people *liked* the reliability of room and board. Lincoln said, "Whenever I hear anyone arguing for slavery, I feel a strong impulse to see it tried on him personally."

He was asked to define tact, "It is the ability to describe others as they see themselves." Rather than complain about a bad cup of coffee he said, "If this is the coffee, please bring me some tea; but if this is the tea, please bring me some coffee." Against jokes about his height he offered a lesson: "You have to do your own growing no matter how tall your grandfather was." Communication is the biggest challenge most leaders have. Lincoln liked candor: "Those who write clearly have readers, those who write obscurely have commentators."

How do you defend staff members under attack? After General Ulysses Grant won several battles he was criticized for drinking. Lincoln acknowledged the complaint and demolished it. "I wish some of you would tell me the brand of whiskey that Grant drinks. I would like to send a barrel of it to my other generals."

How do you find something good to say about a squabbling staff? Lincoln's observation was that, "No matter how much cats fight there always seems to be plenty of kittens." On Lying: "No man has a good enough memory to be a successful liar." On Power: "Nearly all men can stand adversity, but if you want to test a man's character, give him power."

In late 1862 Lincoln grew increasingly frustrated by the refusal of his General of the Army to attack: "If General McClellan isn't going to use his army, I'd like to borrow it for a time."

SPORTS LEADERSHIP

With 2.1 seconds to go in the 1992 NCAA East Regional Championship Game, Duke was one point behind the basketball juggernaut from the University of Kentucky. They had the ball but had to inbound it at the opposite end of the court. Coach Mike Krzyzewski ("Coach K") huddled his team and called the only play that might work. It was, quite literally a long shot. The story I heard about what "Coach K" said goes as follows:

"Grant (Hill) you pass the ball to Chris (Laettner)."

Because of the time left, Grant would have to pass the ball all the way down the court to Chris. If that huge throw worked then Chris would have to turn and fire a jump shot over opposing players instantly. It was the next thing Coach K said that made the difference.

What would you have said next to Laettner? You could say, "Don't miss." What foolish coaching. And yet that is what many leaders tell nurses every single day, "Don't make a medication mistake."

Coach K could have said, "Make it, Chris." Obvious coaching like this insults players. Of course, Chris knows he has to make it. Or he could have said what I would have said, "Chris, we believe in you." But, Coach K's next comment has impacted the world of coaching leadership. He said nothing to Chris. Instead, he turned to the team. "After Chris makes the shot," he said, "the rest of you get back and get your hands up."

With two seconds on the clock, Grant Hill threw the ball the length of the court. With a ridiculous two-tenths of a second left, Christian Laettner's jumper split the net. It is considered the best clutch shot in the best college basketball game in college history.

Coach K's brilliant choice of words *assumed success*. One year before, he had coached Duke to a last second victory over number one UNLV in the semi-finals. Who sank the winning free throws? Christian Laettner. But it is Coach K who has led the big game victories over and over. He continues to offer the kind of leadership that has made both him and Duke basketball legendary.

Too many health care environments are rife with negativity, fear of mistakes and leaders who are chronically risk-averse. Positive encouragement and enlightened leadership brings forth better energy than do fear-driven approaches.

If Moses, Jesus and Mohammed engaged positive hope and radical love to lead their followers why not us? If Lincoln engaged positive energy to fuel the power of a nation why don't we?

Positivity is a life energy open to you. Positivity also informs loving leadership strategy. Become a beacon of hope to yourself and to all you serve.

The Sixth Power
PRESENCE

Your sixth dinner is hosted by a transcendent woman whose birth name meant, "little flower." In fact, Anjezë Gonxhe Bojaxhiu never reached five feet. Yet, she grew so tall that, by the time of her passing, the entire world could see her rising clearly above the crowd.

The little flower, born in 1910, bloomed into a girl deeply in love with her father. She admired him and he doted on her.

At age eight, her father died. Anjeze was bereft. Four years later, though still a young girl, she was present enough to hear her first call to ministry. At eighteen she left home to join the Sisters of Loreto as a missionary. She never saw her mother and sister again. As a nun, she spent her days in prayer and contemplation. Most of all, she cultivated presence to God.

If God is love, presence to others starts with presence to God. On September 10, 1946, the nun's patience was rewarded. Mother Teresa heard what she described as "the call within the call"—a message so deep and penetrating that it led her to a profound promise: "To serve the poorest of the poor."

Service to the poor was a common focus of missionaries. But, in the caste system of India, there were some so poor that they were considered "untouchables"—damned by the gods and not worthy of any attention, much less touching. Suffering and starving in the back streets of India, these degraded fellow beings often died young because no one would hire them, clothe them, house them, or tend to them.

Mother Teresa said that, "she followed Jesus into the slums." There, she offered not only food and water to the poorest of the poor. She offered them her deep and loving presence.

> *Life is a dream, realize it.*
>
> Mother Teresa

After initial resistance, Teresa received Vatican permission and founded a group of sisters named, Missionaries of Charity. Its mission was to care for, as she said, "the hungry, the naked, the homeless, the crippled, the blind, the lepers; all those people who feel unwanted, unloved, uncared for throughout society, people that have become a burden to the society and are shunned by everyone."

The group started with thirteen members. It grew to forty-five hundred. It impacted thousands in Calcutta and millions around the world. Once again, a tiny group had changed the world. And it happened because of what Teresa heard when she was present enough to receive her calling, and to follow it.

Mother Teresa understood that outer presence was deeply influenced by her nun's understanding of mission. This is how she wanted each sister to be experienced by those she served: "...Let the sick and suffering find in her a real angel of comfort and consolation. Let the little ones of the streets cling to her because she reminds them of [Jesus], the friend of the little ones." Only deep presence can project a sense of "comfort and consolation" to the sick and dying.

There can be a painful price for presence as deep as Mother Teresa's. Notice the poison that sometimes drenched her soul. Hear the unquenched desire that tore her heart. She confessed it to Jesus in her diary:

"Lord, my God, who am I that You should forsake me? The Child of your Love and now become as the most hated one, the one You have thrown away as unwanted, unloved. I call, I cling, I want and there is no One to answer, no One on Whom I can cling no, No One. Alone."

This woman, now beatified by the Catholic Church on her path to possible sainthood, had "followed Jesus into the slums." Now, doubt gnawed at her resolve:

"Where is my Faith? Even deep down right in there is nothing, but emptiness and darkness. My God how painful is this unknown pain. I have no Faith. I dare not utter the words and thoughts that crowd in my heart and make me suffer untold agony."

Mother Teresa prevailed as she turned her heart back to those who so desperately needed her radical loving leadership. In some ways, she captures every essence of Radical Loving Care in these stirring lines attributed to her:

Life is an opportunity, benefit from it.
Life is beauty, admire it.
Life is a dream, realize it
Life is a challenge, meet it.
Life is a duty, complete it.
Life is a game, play it.
Life is a promise, fulfill it.
Life is sorrow, overcome it.

Using the power of rhythm Churchill engaged so well, she continues:
Life is a song, sing it.
Life is a struggle, accept it.
Life is a tragedy, confront it.
Life is an adventure, dare it.
Life is luck, make it.
Life is too precious, do not destroy it.
Life is life, fight for it."

Presence means *showing up with your best self*. You do this most powerfully for others with the example you set. You arrive at high presence by considering your example, cultivating your deepest intentions and by practice.

What kind of life should we be present to? Here is Mother Teresa's insight on what will be asked (or not asked) after our life ends: "God will not ask: How many good things have you done in your life?' rather he will ask, 'How much love did you put into what you did?"

"Love begins with a smile," Teresa said. Real presence brings real love. Example energizes behavior. Practice what you preach. Practice promotes power.

SMALL STAGE EXAMPLE—
TWO WORDS THAT CHANGED TWO LIVES

When my son was six weeks old I asked our minister if he could offer parenting advice.

"We could take an hour in my office," he said. "But, I can summarize all my advice in two words. The first one is example. Your example will teach more powerfully than any words you ever say."

"What is the second word," I asked.

"I'll tell you that after you've thought about the first one for a month."

My reflections led me to the example my own fine father, a lifelong leader in the YMCA, set for me. I watched him preach exercise and saw him practice it all the time. I watched him conduct meetings. I do not remember many of his words, but I saw the confidence he generated when he spoke to his staff.

When I looked at my little son I thought about behaviors I wanted to practice in front of him, and what I did not. Of course, I failed to set a good example many times. Still, more than forty years later I have been grateful to see both my children become wonderful and successful members of society and terrific parents.

A month later I asked the minister for the second word.

"Presence," he told me.

"But, I'm a busy lawyer," I told him. "I cannot be with him nearly as much as I would like."

"Presence is not about the *amount* of time you spend with him," he said. "Presence means giving him your complete attention when you *are* with him. Don't look over his head at the television. Look him right in the eyes. Ask him questions. Listen to his answers. Listen to him. Just listen."

This may seem obvious but I found it life-changing. When he was only five years old I would ask my son what he thought I should do in a given criminal case. Even at that age, asking advice signals trust. Today, he is a successful Boston trial attorney. So was my daughter before she became an award-winning photojournalist and then a full time mother.

Clearly, parent examples and full presence do not always work. Luck plays a role. But your children are always watching your example. So is your staff.

Too many leaders (like too many parents) signal "do what I say, not what I do." Instead of being fully present, too many leaders conduct one-on-one meetings by talking *at* staff people instead of listening to their ideas. I have made this mistake too often myself. As for practice, it does not ,of course, make perfect. It is, however, essential for peak performance.

Too many of us are bereft of new ideas because we spend our days consumed with what is right in front of us. The fog of endless meetings obscures what really counts.

Because your first line staff is consumed with immediate needs part of your responsibility is to step back and take a longer view, to plan for improvements. Too many leaders fail at this. One vice president described the failure of his own CEO by saying sarcastically, "Bob's vision is about twenty minutes long."

I know Bob and this was true of him. Instead of serving his followers by climbing the mountains to look ahead, he stayed stuck at ground level. Thus, he pilfered hope's energy from his staff.

In Sports: The Athlete's Focus

Success in sports requires exceptional presence to the moment. Endless practice enables a high focus when it matters most. Back in the days when Tiger Woods was winning golf tournaments right and left a friend saw him capture the top spot at the Memorial Golf Tournament in Columbus.

> *Give me six hours to chop down a tree and I will spend the first four sharpening the axe.*
>
> Abe Lincoln

My friend watched Tiger collect his trophy and prize money. Later on, as he walked to his car, he looked over at the practice tee. Only one golfer was hitting balls. It was Tiger. Instead of heading home to celebrate, the man who had just won it all was already back on the practice tee. (Note that when Tiger's game turned south it was not because he lost the ability to play great golf. It was because he became immersed in domestic trouble that challenged his high purpose focus.)

Every top athlete and leader personifies a key dictate: Be *completely present to your performance*. Practice persistently and you will become better and better—or you will know it is time to change roles. Avoid burnout by cultivating a balanced perspective informed by humor and the arts as well as intensity.

As Lincoln said, sharpen the axe before you cut. Practice over and over and learn something each time. Every fine leader must, like Lincoln, know how to make a joke and take one. They know that humor energizes. Leaders know to take their work seriously, not themselves.

You can learn outer presence from doctors and nurses. Professionals are *always* practicing their profession. Radical Loving Leaders bring radical presence to their work.

The Seventh Power
PEACE

For your final evening with a Radical Loving Leader who changed the world cross the ocean to India. Time-travel back four hundred years.

Members of the British East India Company stepped off their ships and into a land they would subsequently rule, often with an iron hand, for hundreds of years.

Across the decades the members of the relatively small island nation of Britain would win wars against India's people and impose their will and their language on a nation of hundreds of millions. A distinct minority, they would nevertheless rule India for generations. In fact, one of the often-overlooked stories in world history is how much of the world speaks English because of the persistent success of relatively small Great Britain in extending its empire. In the early twentieth century one could say that, "the sun never sets on the British Empire."

> *If there is no struggle, there is no progress.*
>
> Frederick Douglass.

One humble man would change that. On October 2, 1869, four and a half years after the death of Lincoln an Indian woman named Putlibai laid back in a dark windowless room and gave birth to a son of light.

That light did not rise quickly. In school, Putlibai's son did poorly. One report card referred to him as "good at English, fair in Arithmetic and weak in Geography; conduct very good, bad handwriting." Physically small, his sports performance was as pathetic as his academic work. His school performance grew worse after he married at age thirteen. At fifteen, his first child was born by his sixteen-year-old wife, Kasturba. Three days later, the baby died. Eventually, the man who become an idol to his people, would father four children.

By the late 1880s, the young father who had been a poor student had persevered magnificently. Against threats of excommunication from his community, he traveled to England to study law. In June, 1891, Mohandus Gandhi, the man who would one day free India, was called to the bar.

No sooner did Gandhi launch his legal career in Bombay than he ran headlong into a strange obstacle that doomed his potential career as a trial lawyer. When he attempted to cross-examine witnesses he found himself tongue-tied and paralyzed. This man of peace could not bear to make opposing witness uncomfortable!

Gandhi moved to British-controlled South Africa. Over the next twenty-one years he faced brutal discrimination. Some of his experience echoes the Rosa Parks incident. One day, after boarding a train and sitting in the first class section, he was thrown off. The next day, travelling by stagecoach, the driver attacked and beat him for refusing to give his seat to a European passenger. He continued his travels but was refused the right to stay in hotels along the way. On another occasion a white South African suddenly turned on him and beat him bloody because he resented that a "coolie" was walking too close to him.

Gandhi refused to press charges. Throughout these indignities he refused violence of any kind and sustained his inner peace.

These experiences reshaped Gandhi's life and birthed in him the burning passion to bring justice to South Africa. It was not until 1994 that another Radical Loving Leader, Nelson Mandela, won a free election and ended the discriminatory practice of apartheid in South Africa.

Gandhi failed in South Africa. He succeeded in India against persistent efforts by the British to degrade and humiliate him. But, it took Gandhi a quarter century of courageous and peaceful leadership before the violent British yielded to the leadership of the peaceful lawyer who was too kind to cross-examine witnesses.

Seventy-eight years after his birth in the windowless room, Gandhi's Radical Loving Leadership opened a new door through which more than three hundred million Indians walked. The movement he fathered would succeed without a single supporter raising a single sword or firing a single weapon.

Mahatma Gandhi was one of most successful political and spiritual leaders in history. Because he was the modern founder of non-violence as a protest strategy he is also an indirect father of the American Civil Rights Movement.

His sense of purpose, to free the oppressed from segregation and degradation, developed early. Although his belief in independence was widely shared he was the one who stepped forward to lead. You would have to look beneath his quiet demeanor to discover Gandhi's passionate sense of purpose. Look at pictures of him and you might guess he was a street vendor not a world leader.

Gandhi's positive powers are discerned not just through his sense of humor but by watching how he nurtured the flame of hope in millions. His presence to individuals and to vast crowds reflects a classic example of charisma, the kind that can only arise from inner peace. And that is where the small-statured Gandhi stands the tallest.

Raised a Hindu, Gandhi respected all religions as spokes of a wheel with God at the center. When asked about Christianity, however, he looked around at his British oppressors, all Christians. They had beaten and tortured both him and his followers. "Jesus is ideal and wonderful," he reportedly said. "But, I wish I could meet a Christian who actually lived by Jesus' teachings."

Because many believe he was among the most peaceful leaders of all time, a man who would literally accept abuse without striking back and a man who actually prayed for his enemies, some think he was a better "Christian" then most Christians.

On the evening of January 30, 1948, Mahatma Gandhi climbed the steps of a temple to join a prayer service. Nathuram Godse, a nationalist who opposed Gandhi's leadership of peace and tolerance, climbed the same steps and approached the man who had freed India.

At 5:17 p.m. Godse confronted Gandhi. "Brother, Bapu is already late," one of Gandhi's followers told him.

Seconds later Godse raised his Beretta M-1934 semi-automatic pistol and fired three bullets into Gandhi's chest. "Hey Rama" (Oh God) the great leader said, sustaining his sense of peace to the moment of death.

It was less than a year after the British had released their vice grip on the land of three hundred forty million. The man of peace lay dead only a few feet from a place of peace.

Gandhi's legacy is one of the best examples of the power of love-based leadership over violent action. Imagine the millions that were saved because Gandhi equipped his vast "army" with the tools of peace instead of the weapons of war.

Again, what if Martin Luther King, Jr. had armed his followers instead of modeling Gandhi's example? What if all the world chose to resolve conflict by leading from inner peace instead of through violent wars?

It is to Gandhi that we owe the words "Be the change you want to see in the world." It is he who also reminded us of a great truth undergirding inner peace: "The weak can never forgive. Forgiveness is the attribute of the strong." And in a classic comment on the role of love versus fear-based revenge he pointed out that, "An eye for an eye only ends up making the world blind."

Gandhi's advice to all of us lands best in hearts of caregivers: "The best way to find yourself is to lose yourself in the service of others."

Gandhi even defined a key element of Radical Loving Leadership when he wrote that, "Power is of two kinds. One is obtained by the fear of punishment and the other by acts of love. Power based on love is a thousand times more effective and permanent then the one derived from fear of punishment."

Perhaps most useful of all is the quote we can apply so well to ourselves. "My life is my message," Gandhi said. What a message he has left for all of us.

VIOLENCE AGAINST THE PEACEFUL

Remarkably, three of our radical loving leaders, Lincoln, Gandhi, and Martin Luther King, met violent deaths at the hands of assassins with guns. Each of them gave their lives for justice.

Of the four remaining, Frankl escaped a violent death, according to his own report, by luck and fate.

On February 15, 1933, Giuseppe Zangara fired five shots at Franklin Roosevelt. He missed FDR but killed Chicago mayor Anton Cermak.

The Nazis so feared the power of Churchill's leadership that they developed a plan to defeat Britain by assassinating him. Their plot was to hide explosives inside chocolate. The plot, of course, melted into failure.

There are no reports of any attempts on the life of the gentle Mother Teresa.

Inner peace promises outer success. In fact, inner peace is the *only* way to ensure success in the world. When you have it, you are equipped to stand strong on the shifting sands of the earth.

Inner peace is the compass, your soul's North Star.

Every great leader leads from inner peace.

Every successful leader projects a presence that comes from an inner peace

THE DOWNSIDE OF GREATNESS

Do not be too moral. You may cheat yourself out of much life so. Aim above morality. Be not simply good; be good for something.

Henry David Thoreau

All great leaders need to be seen in perspective. Their genius does not shield them from flaws. Like Achilles, each of them had vulnerabilities. It is important to scale them back to life size.

Passionate people are deeply in touch with their feelings. They soar to heights we do not reach and lift us part way with them. They can also sink into darkness. Many high successes have been ripped by bipolar disorder.

All seven of the heroes we celebrate were stalked by what Churchill called "his black dog." That is why the attendant power of persistence is so important.

Another downside lives in sometimes "scandalous" behavior. Roosevelt and King engaged in affairs and King reportedly plagiarized parts of his doctoral thesis. Churchill was often a raging drunk. Lincoln was sometimes as irritable as a gored bull.

Gandhi, the great proponent of non-violence, admits in his autobiography that he once beat his wife, Kasturba. Some thought it was a scandal when, after Mother Teresa's death, it was discovered in her private journals that she had doubted God.

LEADERSHIP AND RUBBER DUCKS

How can private indiscretion undermine public leadership? How ridiculous can it get? Fifty years after the fact, NBC News revealed on February 8, 2012, one of the odder scandals to strike a famous leader. If this story had come out during John F. Kennedy's Presidency it might have sunk his career. The details may provide as much humor as they do teaching.

Mimi Alford was a twenty-year-old White House intern. She was also one of JFK's mistresses.

> *I'm a human being and I fall in love and I don't have control of every situation.*
>
> Beyoncé

On air, Ms. Alford revealed, credibly, that our then Commander- in-Chief, "...had a collection of little yellow rubber ducks and they were in the bathtub and rubber ducks sort of became part of our game."

The hero of PT 109 in WW II had become the admiral of a fleet of rubber ducks. While world events swirled outside, the leader of the free world held duck races in the bathtub with his paramour. (Of course, as we saw with President Bill Clinton and other top leaders across our history, Kennedy's case is not isolated.)

Imagine if during the duck games in 1962 an agent had knocked on the bathroom door to warn the President of an imminent Soviet attack: "Toy Ducks Sink Kennedy," a headline might have read. It would be reminiscent of Nero fiddling while Rome burned.

The great leaders deliver endless riches to us. When these leaders misbehave, some people act like they deserve a complete refund and the wrong-acting leader should be banished to the ash can of history. Beyonce may be able to "lose control" in certain situations. Leaders are punished for such "human" mistakes.

It is a tragedy that Lance Armstrong destroyed his legacy by cheating. It is also a tragedy that so much of the great work he did with his Live Strong effort has been tossed aside. Former Senator John Edwards ruined his own promising career. But, do we have to let his errors obscure his purposeful focus on poverty in America? Sometimes, an old and tired phrase applies, "don't throw out the baby with the bath water." The baby is too important. (Or, in Kennedy's case, "Don't throw out the President with the rubber ducks.")

A SIDE NOTE:
CHURCHILL AND GANDHI AT PEACE

Some of the seven leaders profiled here were in conflict with each other. Anxious to preserve the British Empire, Churchill opposed Gandhi's goal of independence. It was not Churchill's finest hour.

A fascinating decision has juxtaposed these two giants in death. A nine and a half foot statue of Gandhi now stands in a London park. Twice the size of the living Gandhi, it looms nearby another longstanding statue of his opponent, Winston Churchill.

Part Three

The Practices

Applying The Seven Powers

The dogmas of the quiet past are inadequate to the stormy present. The occasion is piled high with difficulty and we must rise with the occasion. As our case is new, we must think anew and act anew. We must disenthrall ourselves, and then we shall save our country.

Abraham Lincoln

A STARTING MODEL IN BRIEF

Men [sic] have become the tools of their tools.

Henry David Thoreau

Some like lists. The point of this entire section is to focus on ways you can implement the seven powers. Here is a summary model that you, as a healthcare leader can follow as one way to engage Radical Loving Leadership. Here is what the great leaders understand:

Vision: "We will ensure that every leader and caregiver passes The Mother Test."

Leadership Structure: Set up a leadership group to oversee and drive the vision.

Accountability: Put your vision at the top of the agenda for every meeting.

Priorities: Note what determines culture and make changes to align every function with Mother Test priorities. Build a culture where peer pressure affirms excellence.

Hiring and Assigning: Hire for a Servant's Heart. Hiring, promoting and assigning the right people to the right roles are among the biggest determinants of success. A coach who recruits the best and positions them right is seventy-five percent of the way to success.

Orientation: Adopt the IIF (Inspiration, Information & Fun) strategy. Make orientation inspirational and fun as well as informational.

Team Strength: After new employees leave an energizing orientation they need to enter a strong team. Positive leaders energize. Negative leaders kill success.

Training: Put The Mother Test at the center of training. Remember that The Mother Test applies to how leaders treat *caregivers* as well as how caregivers treat patients.

Staff Reviews: Determine which of your staff can pass The Mother Test, who fails, and who is drifting in between. What will you do about this? If you have people you do not want caring for your mother why are they there? Embed the concept of Radical Loving Care into staff reviews.

Difficult Conversations: Use Radical Loving Care to train staff how to handle layoffs and terminations.

Rounding: Strengthen rounding frequency and skills. Recognize rounding as a way to raise energy. Ask the number one best question: How do you give loving care?

Affirmation: Encourage, affirm, reward, catch your staff being good and celebrate it.

LEADERSHIP VERSUS FIRST LINE WORK

As radical loving leader Jason Barker says, "leadership requires a radically different set of skills than direct task work." Success relies heavily on your relationship abilities, your intuition and other hard to measure traits.

Accountants are trained in accounting, not leadership. Intuition did not win them their CPA. Plumbers are trained to fix pipes, not lead other plumbers. Nurses are trained to deliver medications and give nursing care. They are not trained to lead.

In fact, most leaders have *never* been trained to lead. Oddly, it is assumed they already know. To lead well, every leader must create a new story of what that means.

Absent a meaningful story the quotidian routines that are endemic to hospitals can birth soul-killing language. In referring

> *Maturity calls us to risk ourselves as much as immaturity, but for a bigger picture...*
> *not for gains that make us smaller.*
>
> David Whyte

to the need to cut staff, a finance officer reported, "We've got 3,468 units of expense. If we cut the right one hundred units we would save millions." He was, unfortunately, talking about the number of employees.

One Chief Operating Officer, facing the prospect of lay-offs, referred to "the number of bodies we need to eliminate." It is common (and I have done it often myself) to refer to numbers of associates as FTEs (Full time equivalent employees.)

This is language that can dehumanize health care.

Loving leadership cannot be doled out in milligrams or cubic centimeters. Martin Luther King did not write his success with spreadsheets. New leadership training needs to engage human psychology as well as teaching how to create a strategic plan.

Everyone needs to learn how to communicate with stories. As Anatole Broyard wrote, "Whether he (or she) wants to be or not, the doctor is a storyteller and he (or she) can turn our lives into good or bad stories, regardless of the diagnosis."

Your stories signal what you value. Every good coach knows that. Every good politician knows that.

Many healthcare leaders do not.

The First Power
APPLYING PURPOSE

Purpose is present and may be woven into everything we do.

Olivia McIvor, *Turning Compassion Into Action*

Do you ever think of the caregivers that came before you, of the housekeeper who spent her days clearing sheets off beds, of the nurse who spent her nights helping patients into and out of bed, of the physical therapist who walked stroke patients through the endless patterns of rehabilitation?

Do you ever imagine the leaders who headed off to the place you work every morning, the ghosts who traveled the hallways before you and whose steps you walk in today? What of the guidance they gave, the plans they drew up, the inspiration they offered and the curved tables they sat around to discuss what would happen in those days?

> *What are we afraid of, what stops us from speaking out and claiming the life we want for ourselves? Quite often it is a sudden horrific understanding of the intimate and extremely personal nature of the exploration.*
>
> David Whyte

What fields have your predecessors plowed and fertilized for you? How well are you doing harvesting the wisdom of your long line of predecessors? What will your successors draw from the legacy of *your* leadership?

Victor Frankl teaches that a purposeful vision comes first. His vision was to survive the concentration camp so that he could see his wife and write the words that are yet read today.

Since Love is the highest power and purpose we know, *why not engage love in your everyday work?* If you could engage Love's power at a higher level, what would your life look like?

Frankl's case is offered as an extreme to penetrate our thinking. He wrote about his wife. But, *wherever love goes energy flows.*

Consider the way the mother image evokes love. What have countless soldiers cried out for after being wounded on the battlefield? They scream for the personification of love. In their agony and fear they shriek, "Mother!"

"Where life [had] gone stale, transfiguration occurs," John O'Donohue wrote. Amid your reflection and looking through new eyes you may notice important corners of your being where the breath of your life has gone stale. "Transfiguration" awaits the oxygen of your deeper breaths.

PROFILE OF PURPOSE

Give yourself time to let a yes resound within you. When it's right, I guarantee that your entire body will feel it

Oprah Winfrey.

On a spring Saturday in Fort Lauderdale decades ago a young woman plugged lines into the switchboard at Imperial Point Hospital, making connections between callers and patients, among doctors and patients and among leaders and the led.

She is still connecting people to people, but now it is on a far vaster scale. From her job as a hospital switchboard operator all those years ago Nancy Schlichting has risen to become President and CEO of the giant, Detroit-based Henry Ford Health System.

Nancy has painted a leadership masterpiece on the canvas of high purpose. Under her guidance, Henry Ford has become a 4.7 billion dollar system with 24,000 employees, including 1300 employed physicians and researchers.

"My purpose has always been focused on people... I believe my job as CEO is to create a great environment for all people to reach their full potential... this includes patients, employees and physicians," Schlichting says. "I have done this by embracing diversity and embracing community to fully leverage the assets of health care organizations to improve health and wellness, one person at a time. I have also been passionate about creating a culture of "yes" to drive innovation, speaking up, and inclusion."

A culture of "yes" is one of keys that opened the door to Nancy's leadership success. Across her many years as a radical loving leader (at organizations including Riverside Methodist Hospital where we worked together) she has illuminated loving purpose in hundreds of thousands of lives, "one person at a time," with her culture of "yes."

How do you lead organizations to greatness? You start with a sterling purpose. Follow Nancy's advice and open your heart to "yes." Persist to success.

Love alone is capable of uniting living beings in such a way as to complete and fulfill them, for it alone takes them and joins them by what is deepest in themselves.

Pierre Teilhard de Chardin

Everyone in a healthcare organization, from nurse to plumber, from doctor to CEO, from accountant to admitting clerk, is a caregiver. Radical loving leaders unite everyone around a common purpose that lives "deepest in themselves."

If you work in Accounts Receivable your "patients" are your fellow caregivers. If you work in medical staff support your "patients" may be physicians. If you are a leader your "patients," of course, are employees.

Patients and fellow employees test your ability to love every day. Sometimes cranky, non-compliant, or insolent, you may wonder how you can possibly "love" such people. Yet, that is what The Mother Test calls you to do, to love at the hardest times as well as at the easiest.

As a caregiver, patients are no longer strangers.

LIFT UP PURPOSE IN A CLEAR WAY.

Look how simple it is to frame the goals of the great. Martin Luther King's vision was to integrate the south. Franklin Roosevelt's during his first and second term was to defeat the Great

> *First make sure that what you aspire to accomplish is worth accomplishing, and then throw your whole vitality into it.*
>
> Publisher B.C. Forbes

Depression and restore the nation to economic stability. During his third and fourth terms it was to save democracy against the Axis powers.

Churchill's vision was not only to save England but western civilization itself. Lincoln's was to unite the nation and eliminate slavery. Frankl's was to prove the importance of meaning in life. To say "yes."

Mother Teresa spoke her vision in a few words: "To serve the poorest of the poor." She and her fellow nuns found them in India. Before Teresa, Gandhi's was to free India from British rule.

THE FLAT VISION

What visions fall flat? "This place ain't broke so let's don't fix it." As uninspiring as that sounds that is exactly the way most leaders do their job. Some leaders at Riverside Methodist Hospital actually told me that when I arrived in 1983: "Erie, you got a great job. This place ain't broke. No fixing needed."

This was partly true. Riverside Methodist was stable and above average. The problem was that it was resting on its laurels. You cannot maintain the status quo in a changing world if you only seek to perpetuate the past.

CLIMB THE MOUNTAIN

In the year after President Thomas Jefferson completed the largest acquisition of territory in the history of our country, before or since, he ordered two Army officers to lead a death-defying exploration. Jefferson set the vision as clearly as he could, "The object of your mission is to explore the Missouri River, & such principle stream of it, as, by its course and communication with the waters of the Pacific ocean, whether the Columbia, Oregon, Colorado or any other river may offer the most direct & practicable water communication across this continent for the purpose of commerce." Essentially, their charge was to find and map a Northwest Passage to the Pacific.

In May, 1804, Captain Meriwether Lewis and Second Lieutenant William Clark, together with a few dozen hardy travelers, launched the daunting journey. Lewis and Clark would become one of the most famous duos in American history.

Traveling new ground they often felt lost. Engaging the same principles you and any fine leader would use, Lewis and Clark found the best guides they could, like the great Native American Sacajawea. They consulted what maps they had and sent scouts and climbed mountains for a view ahead. Two years and four months later, after traversing largely unknown lands between St. Louis and the Pacific Ocean, they returned. Their original mission, to discover a continuous string of waterways from St. Louis to the Pacific, had failed. Their vast accomplishments became a triumphant demonstration of the power of purpose and how it can motivate a small band to accomplish historic success.

Use *your* "compass" and climb the nearest "mountains" to envision the goal and inspire energy in your followers. In the spirit of Lewis and Clark, lead your group to success. Above all else, establish a vision to "build a cathedral." Fasten each

> *Every patient is someone's mother, sister, brother, father or friend...*
> *Everyone is a caregiver.*

heart in your group to this vision. Transforming your team into a group of energized and dedicated caregivers is as important (and daunting) in its way as exploring a new path to the Pacific. Your leadership job is to keep your group inspired and focused all the way to success.

That is, by analogy, where Riverside Methodist's true success lay: not in the settled land of the present but on the other side of the mountains. We reached the valley where a loving culture was planted and bloomed magnificently. Successors can climb new mountains on the shoulders of the pioneers that went before.

Leaders like Nancy Schlichting watch group behavior: When billing clerks in your new culture think of themselves as caregivers you know you are succeeding. When electricians and cashiers and security officers and information desk clerks and every single leader think of themselves as caregivers and peak performers then you are winning the day.

SKEPTICS VERSUS CYNICS

You will know your vision is bold when the skeptics and the cynics fly out of the woodwork. Lewis and Clark, Columbus, Thomas Edison, Martin Luther King, Jr., Steve Jobs, Bill Gates and The Mayo brothers faced both groups at every step along the way.

Nancy knows that resistance to new journeys is guaranteed. If you do not experience some, you are not pioneering.

She listens to the skeptics. They will have constructive ideas and some of them will be good. She ignores the cynics (or removes them). They never like *anything*. They dislike the status quo and yet they will never support changing it. They cannot be won over.

Cynics are destructive and drag down energy. Constructive skeptics, however, are invaluable.

167

THE "IMPOSSIBLE" PUZZLE

I use a "magic puzzle" to teach purpose, persistence and positive leadership. The puzzle looks impossible but it can be solved. When I offer it to groups I do not say whether this tough puzzle can be done.

The last time I tried this with a large leadership team one of the small groups of six dropped out fast. A classic cynic had taken charge. After a brief effort the team looked frustrated. The cynic offered quick relief, "This is a trick. This puzzle cannot be solved."

Anxious to escape their frustration, the group bought this exit strategy immediately. Five of the six remaining members quit working.

When I swore to the group that the puzzle could be solved and *would* be solved, the cynic said, "Don't listen to him." And they did not.

Twenty minutes later another group solved the puzzle, then another and another until every team had succeeded except the team that quit. Predictably, the cynic refused to accept responsibility. "You guys didn't have to listen to me," he told his frustrated team members.

Pioneers keep trying. It is impossible for quitters to succeed because they refuse to finish the job.

Even among your best team members, and perhaps in your own heart, doubt will nag at your energy. That is why it is so critical that you keep nurturing your own purpose.

THE MOTHER TEST AS A VISION AGAINST A CERTAIN MADNESS

If you pick it and pursue The Mother Test you will transform every life you touch. Simply say: "Our vision is to pass The Mother Test." Engage as many as possible to shape it. When it is shaped, share it in every way you can. Rebuild your team to fit the new vision.

Embed short-term goals early. As you plant the vision and dig deeper into the problem you may discover a certain madness in the way things have been. You may wonder, as you look into the shadows, why your organization has hosted so many subpar caregivers and leaders for so long.

King picked the right team to beat back bigotry. Gandhi announced the strategy of non-violent resistance when he could easily have called his followers to arms against the vastly outnumbered British. Roosevelt set up the government agencies that would solve infrastructure problems while simultaneously easing joblessness against a backdrop of desolation.

Engage for yourself King's "tough-minded and tender-hearted thinking." There is nothing loving about being nice   to your staff and then delivering incompetent direction. Conversely, there is nothing loving about fixing the balance sheet while treating your staff like objects instead of people.

What lives on the other side of the tangled forest that grows between you and success? Sit back in your office and thumb through policies and budgets, sit in meeting after meaningless meeting, terrorize your staff with budget demands, and your team members will plod along like whipped oxen, and never share their best gifts.

Or get out there and live loving leadership.

THE FIVE RINGS IN THE PATIENT-CENTERED CIRCLE: DREAMING AND DOING

> *If you can dream it you can do it*
>
> Walt Disney

Dream of a better day for you and for all those around you. In the safety of your dreams you, as a leader, can be daring, even "crazy."

Sigmund Freud suggested that dreams are often most profound when they seem the most crazy. Convert "profound" to "life-changing."

You are not going to move your team forward by dreaming small.

There is nothing loving about being nice to a patient and then delivering incompetent care. Conversely, there is nothing loving about "fixing a patient's problem" while treating them like an object instead of a person. I would never have been successful as a trial lawyer or healthcare CEO if all I had done was act "nice." Conversely, I would have failed if I had just been a tough guy.

Thousands of healthcare leaders have learned that Radical Loving Care is the kind of care you want for your mother *and* for yourself. Many have transformed the places they lead into centers of healing.

Pictures help too—if they are simple.

When we took over the Baptist Hospital System in 1998 it was clear the organization had lost focus as well as money. Thirty million dollars had been squandered in an ill-fated investment in a Medicaid-style insurance company. Millions more were being spent on sponsoring sports teams.

What about patient care? I drew a circle on a flip chart. I put a "P" (standing for patient) at the center. Leadership had forgotten their mission. This is the most powerful leadership drawing I ever offered:

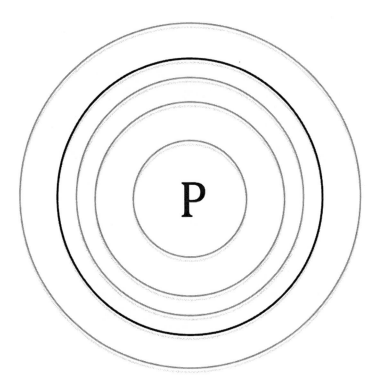

Imagine the caregiving model as a group of concentric circles. In the middle of the circle is the "P" for patient.

FIRST RING: The first ring *around* the patient is made up of direct caregivers. Because hospitals were established to care for the sick and wounded, physicians, therapists and nurses have long been the first ring caregivers.

SECOND RING: These are also direct service providers. They include first line leaders as well as support staff who maintain equipment, finance staff who look after expenses and income, pay vendors, bring crucial equipment and administer the all-important system that delivers paychecks. They directly support the first ring.

THIRD RING: Senior executives and CEOs may think of themselves as big shots. But, they actually work in the third circle. That is why their most important job is to *take care of the people who take care of people*, to support the first and second line staff that is closer to the patient.

And that is why executives also need to support and attend to the needs of the most highly-skilled people in the building, the physicians who admit patients and the specialists who perform highly-sophisticated care.

It is primarily the job of the CEO and his team to ensure that the hospital is staffed with the finest physicians possible. It is very difficult to travel the full path to excellence with anything less.

FOURTH RING: In the fourth ring are peripheral activities remote from patient care. Some hospitals have too much energy invested in these. As mentioned, when I took over the beleaguered Baptist Hospital System in Nashville, the hospital owned a major interest in a Medicaid insurance company and was spending millions each year sponsoring sports teams.

FIFTH RING: In the fifth ring is the Board of Directors. The boards of America's hospitals have a solemn responsibility, the responsible stewardship of organizations they oversee. Their most important decision is the selection of a CEO and their oversight of that person's performance.

The area outside the rings is the community at large. Looking at the hospital from the outside, they are the ones who count on your organization as a crucial asset in their region.

The better health care systems, like ProMedica based in Toledo, Ohio led by Randy Oostra, go beyond the inpatient mission and into the community. They recognize the enormous impact that food and fitness have on illness. They actively promote good health including good nutrition and better food for the poor because they know this is also part of their mission. And they signal that message to their sixteen thousand employees so they will know they are part of this solution also.

Radical Loving Leadership must guide each ring. *The CEO must guide the whole circle.* Each group must be on board for everyone to succeed.

Revisit your career commitment. How do you lean into your strength?

Ralph Ellison asks a provocative question in his epic book, *The Invisible Man*: "What and how much had I lost by trying to do only what was expected of me instead of what I myself had wished to do?"

Forget about what others expect of you. What do *you* expect of you? What do you want your life to say over the next years?

THE GOLDEN AGENDA (OR THE LEADEN ONE)

> *Do you manage your agenda or does your agenda manage you?*

If your meeting agendas: 1) look the same all the time, 2) are not moving you forward on your path to radical loving leadership, it is time to adopt The Golden Agenda. This is the agenda in which you are constantly engaging the process of **Idea, Action, and Reflection.**

Offer an idea, like hiring for a Servant's Heart. Put it into action. Reflect on how the idea is working. Make adjustments.

Health care staff members are great at caregiving. Health care leaders (unlike their counterparts at entrepreneurial companies) are terrible at meetings. Every hospital leader will tell you that enormous amounts of time are wasted on over-talking agenda items.

Mark Dissette, a Senior Vice President at Holy Cross Hospital in Ft. Lauderdale, has his team members stand during meeting so that everyone is motivated to stay on the point.

George Mikitarian's staff at Parrish Medical Center holds regular five minute huddles to focus team energy and inspire performance.

When is your regular agenda going to become the basis for action?

YOUR PERSONAL PURPOSE TEST

Do you brace yourself against work or do you *embrace* life?

Is your life dominated by fear or love?

If you answered, "love," then dive deeper. How much are your daily decisions *pulled* by outside fears as opposed to *guided* by love?

> *Moods affect messages. That is why love and professionalism are so important.*

Are you primarily driven by desire or do you lead others with a passion for excellence?

How do Cecil Beaton's words land in your heart? "Be daring, be different, be impractical, be anything that will assert integrity of purpose and imaginative vision against the play-it-safers, the creatures of the commonplace, the slaves of the ordinary."

One leader told me, "Ever since I was a boy I've been told to be practical, careful." Now you are challenged to "be daring, be different, be impractical?" It will take a new brand of leadership for you to raise the caregiving standards around you.

Alternatively, who wants to be seen as a one of the "slaves of the ordinary?"

As a leader, you have far more power than you think you do. Yet, if you are using your power primarily to boss people around do you deserve the power you have? Threatening people to pass The Mother Test does not work. You are promoting loving care, not terror.

As I have said, my heart breaks for any employee who lives in fear of a tyrannical boss. Rehabilitate such leaders or remove them.

How Language Empowers Purpose and Vision

In any given day at Nashville Baptist Hospital in 2001 fourteen babies were born. In that same day, two patients would pass away.

What if you told your staff "that means that every day fourteen people are spending their first day with us. Two are spending their last."

That is the privilege and the responsibility of working in the life and death world of a hospital. Caregivers are present for big life events. Leaders and ancillary staff are there to support these caregivers in their work. All engagements must fuel the core goal of the hospital, patient care.

ARE YOUR PARTNERS ON YOUR PAGE?

"Bob Jefferson" met me in the lobby of the giant Nashville clinic he leads; he met me in the lobby because the waiting room was jammed.

"Look at all those patients," he said proudly. "I love it."

An hour later I hung around after Bob said goodbye. "How are you liking your work today?" I asked the veteran clerk at the front desk.

"I hate it," she said. "Look at all these patients I have to deal with!"

The "treasure" for Bob is a full waiting room showing his clinic is popular and in demand.

The "treasure" for the first line clerk is an *empty* waiting room in which she can rest and go about other duties.

How would you, as the leader, bring your first line staff onto the same page with you? How would you lead them to the point where they are as enthusiastic as are you about celebrating the same treasure of success?

> *Good is not good enough in healthcare because lives and health are at stake.*

Overbearing bosses can force you to *appear* to accept this invitation to excellence. But, they cannot *make you* succeed because they do not know your secret heart.

No one else, not even your boss, will know if you are on board the boat. That is because you and I both know the tricks, how to make it *look* like we're on the trip when really we are just moving our feet.

Victor Frankl's brutal guards could not stop his high-purpose voyage because it was a heart journey. Neither could they invade his rich thoughts or disturb his beautiful longing for his wife.

In this journey you lead with your heart as well as your head. That is why only you will know if you are making genuine progress.

YOUR LEGACY

A strong legacy always flows from a successfully executed purpose driven by a clear vision. What is the legacy of your leadership thus far? As Senator Henry Clay wrote, "The time will come when winter will ask what you were doing all summer."

Resolve anew to lead. Draw an image of your staff. Have you got the right people in the right positions? Do you have people whose strengths offset your weaknesses?

Nancy Schlichting has refused to surround herself with a group of clones. As a radical loving leader she picks team members with complimentary strengths because she knows that a diverse team meets challenges best.

As you convert your story from bland rhyme into inspiring music, a new energy will sing through your life.

> *Once you start doing only what you've already proven you can do, you're on the road to death.*
>
> Comedian Jerry Seinfeld

Create a "self-story" in which you picture yourself as an affirming leader of a team with great potential. Focus your attention on this new story. Everyone will feel your excitement.

The Mother Test is not a game any more than it is a game to treat a person in pain. It is serious work about one of humanity's most important issues—how we care for those who are suffering.

The Mother Test is about holding your team *accountable* to give great care to *every* person – not just patients.

Remember. There is no point in learning new tools if you are what Beaton calls a "slave of the ordinary." If you are reading this only because a leader is making you do it, then the book cannot speak to you. Make this work your own.

THE ENERGY IN A VESSEL OF MEANING

Dr. Frankl proved that the most important vessel is the one filled with meaning. The most powerful source of meaning arises from love.

> *...a person is afraid of growing old to the extent that he is not really living now.*
>
> Dr. Carl Jung

The best thing about love is that it comes to you free. But it is not cheap. There is a terrific reward; the richest life has to offer. Opening yourself as a vessel, Love will enrich your life beyond your wildest dreams.

How did Frankl survive the horrors of Dachau? Love, specifically love for both his wife and his work. That is what saved his life. Love became his daily bread.

I have encountered hundreds of caregivers who have lost the meaning in their daily work. What once seemed like a calling has become drudgery. The bright mornings of their first days of work have become gray afternoons of boredom and meaninglessness.

"How long until Friday?" these caregivers ask themselves on the other weekdays. From there it is a short step to the next question, "How many years before I retire?" Thus, some healthcare workers become caught in a sort of concentration camp. You can see it in their eyes.

Each day for them seems like the next. Each hour is one more step in the meaningless march to the freedom of the weekend or the apparent luxury of retirement. In fact, some leaders have "retired in place," going through the motions when they are no longer truly present.

Dr. Carl Jung believed that "a person is afraid of growing old to the extent that he is not really living now." Want to beat burnout? Embrace your work *now*.

If you do not, each day of work becomes wasted—filled with the empty energy of longing for the future rather than the joy of helping others right now. If work has lost meaning (or you have *never* discovered meaning in your work) how do *you* find the "salvation" Frankl describes? How do you become the vessel Love wants to fill up so that you may pour her into the heart of another?

Love cannot make its way through you unless she is welcomed. She is more likely to come if you, paradoxically, want it for another, not yourself.

One hundred percent of those in depression report that they have lost meaning in their lives. This belief affects their brain chemistry. That is partly why drugs like Prozac work. But, success with such drugs may not be sustainable unless the patient finds their "why."

Meaning gives energy to endure suffering. Your mother may have gone through agony to give birth to you. But her pain was informed by an energy-giving hope—to give *you* life. Meaning can literally imbue people with superhuman strength. A one hundred pound mom can lift a three thousand pound car if her baby is trapped beneath. A man can survive days adrift at sea in a lifeboat if he has hope.

Nietzsche's words echo: "He who has a Why to live for can bear almost any How."

PATTERN SMASHING

You must live in the present, launch yourself on every wave, find your eternity in each moment.

Henry David Thoreau

Many patterns already control your life. Some are good. Some are not only bad but damage you and those around you.

Pattern change is *extremely* difficult. Psychologists believe it happens most effectively in one of four ways: 1) a traumatic event causing quick change, 2) An epiphany, a sudden realization that causes a life change, 3) learning and practicing new patterns, and 4) peer pressure.

Of these, we engage practical learning, practice and peer pressure.

A KEY TOOL: Use affirmation and encouragement to change behavior because affirmation causes leaders to associate new patterns with *pleasure instead of pain.*

If you need to teach a leader to become better at rounding follow them around. Affirm and encourage each positive behavior you see. Do this again and again to reinforce the change. Soon a new and better behavior will emerge.

Cognitive Psychology also teaches that **Four Phases** are part of every meaningful behavioral change.

Consider the extreme of an alcoholic and it will help you understand how your patterns may be as strong as addictions.

1) **Awareness** Most alcoholics are aware that they are drinking too much but they have dismissed this as a problem. They do not accept that their drinking equals alcoholism. This denial blocks change.

2) **Acceptance** Recovering alcoholics have traveled though this stage. They have gone from awareness of their drinking to acceptance of alcoholism, a disease that requires a treatment process.

3) **Vision** In these moments the alcoholic makes a picture of what his or her life would look like without alcohol. Often, this image is too painful and the alcoholic gives up.

When the alcoholic can see his or her new life as one in which alcohol is no longer a jailer the next stage appears.

4) **Action** Success begins when the alcoholic stops drinking. The pain of withdrawal may appear. But the recovering alcoholic learns to hang on. In addition, constant affirmation helps anchor the new behavior.

The process goes in a circle and needs to be constantly nurtured.

HOW ABOUT YOU AND YOUR TEAM?

How about you? Can you clear the deck of all the junk that has been slowing down progress? Compare your own reality to the pattern change process:

AWARENESS: You may be **aware** that your crew is underperforming. You may have decided this is no big deal. You may look around and see that "you're no worse than anyone else" (There's a great standard. "Look at us. We're no worse than anyone else!")

ACCEPTANCE: Accept that your team's average performance is a problem.

VISION: What would we look like if we passed The Mother Test?

ACTION: Put your new vision into **action.** Try it out. Make adjustments. Persist! Use affirmation every step of the way.

THE DOCK, THE BOAT AND IN-BETWEEN

Everyone one who has climbed into a small boat knows they must move from the stability of the dock to the movement in the boat. The dock is solid but the boat's destination offers adventure.

If you do not climb on board, you risk being left behind, permanently. Accordingly, you can stay on the dock or get into the boat. Or you can try the third choice.

> *New programs only work if leaders use new approaches*

You can put one foot in the boat and keep the other on the dock. You cannot, of course, do that very long. You have to move one way or the other or risk falling into the drink.

Imagine that your boss is captain of a ship and he invites you on board. But the ship looks shaky and the path your boss has charted is one you have never taken. You are worried the boat might sink anyone invited on board. The dock feels comfortable to you and you do not want to leave. The horn blows. The ship is about to leave.

Still unsure you put one foot on board and keep one on the dock. You can sustain that pose only until the ship begins to sail.

When I took over Nashville's largest hospital it had more than forty million in operating losses.

The hospital was in such dangerous economic condition that, in 1998, I contacted other health care systems to see if they might either bail us out or actually buy the hospital. Most notably, both Vanderbilt University and Ascension Health, owners of St. Thomas Hospital, declined. My speculation is that they wanted to wait until the hospital went bankrupt and then buy it cheap.

My recollection of a discussion with one Ascension executive is that I warned him about the possibility of a turnaround at Baptist. "If we bring this hospital back, you will find the price has gone up sharply." They decided to take their chances. They decided wrong. Three years later, with Baptist back in the black (though not profitable enough to stand alone) Ascension paid more that $300 million dollars for the system.

But, in 1998, we stood alone. Only bold action could save that venerable ship from sinking. As we developed the plan I gave them the boat analogy. Some stayed on the dock. Some got on board. Many hovered in that awkward spot in between. They were the "wait-and-see" group.

The problem with wait-and-see people is that their energy will be diluted by indecision. Bold leadership can only tolerate diminished energy for so long.

As for those with a foot in both places some fell into the water and drowned. In other words, they were let go.

After the first year at Baptist, everyone saw that we had cut the loss from seventy-three million to thirty million. I held a celebration. "Look," I told our team, "We lost only thirty million!"

Of course, we needed to do much more. Those that we kept on board saw us cut the loss to four million at the end of the next year. By the end of the third year, huge loses had been turned into a one million dollar gain.

Employee and patient satisfaction were sky high. Key medical staff embraced our success. Radical Loving Care was a reality. The Joint Commission toured the hospital and gave us a rating of 98%, almost unheard of for a large hospital.

Most important of all, we were passing The Mother Test.

Our ship had reached a key island in our voyage to success.

The Mother Test is a vision of high purpose. Passing The Mother Test requires changing *the human experience*. Changing the human experience calls for across-the-board *culture change*.

The Second Power
APPLYING PASSION

Wealth is the ability to fully experience life.

Henry David Thoreau

PROFILE IN PASSIONATE LEADERSHIP

The patient was critically ill with congestive heart failure. In fact, all the patients in the unit were critically hill. That is the world of intensive care. That is also the stage in which a young nurse applied her passion for care decades ago.

For ten years as a first line nurse, she took care of patients one at a time. Today, Laurie Harting looks after fourteen thousand caregivers as head of the six-hospital Dignity Health System (Sacramento region).

Laurie loves "The Starfish Effect." She retells the old story of the man watching a woman on a beach covered with thousands of stranded starfish. The woman is picking up the starfish one at a time and throwing them back to the safety of the ocean. "Why are you doing that?" the man asks her, "you cannot possibly save all these starfish."

"I can save this one," the woman said tossing a starfish back into the ocean.

"When I was a frontline nurse, I helped 'starfish' one at a time," Laurie told me. "Now I get to help fourteen thousand 'starfish' care for hundreds of thousands of patients every year."

This is Laurie's third time running hospitals in different parts of the country. Each time, she has brought radical loving care to the fore by practicing radical loving leadership. The second winner of the national Healing Hospital award, she keeps advancing to larger and larger roles because she is so darn successful. Now she is one of the top healthcare leaders in America.

The Starfish story reinforces the exponential power you have to influence the lives of others. What ripples will flow from the actions you take this morning? Which starfish can you save today? Laurie Harting says that it is up to you.

In the classic film, "It's A Wonderful Life" Jimmy Stewart decides he does not just *like* Donna Reed. He *loves* her. Put aside ideas about what you like and *embrace what you love.*

King was passionate about integrating the south. Become passionate about passing The Mother Test.

Excessive rule-following kills passion. There are new guidelines in a culture of excellence. They are not hard and fast rules.

Janet, a chief nursing officer at a large hospice, awoke one night in terrible pain. As a nurse, she worried she might be having a heart attack or, at least, a kidney stone. In any case, she believed her very life was at risk.

Her husband rushed her to the hospital emergency department. He pulled up outside the entrance, ran inside and called out to the nearest nurse, "My wife thinks she is having a heart attack. Come quick please."

The first line nurse grabbed a nearby wheelchair and headed towards the exit door. A supervisor shouted, "No wheelchairs outside the ER."

The nurse was stunned. The husband was horrified as was a nearby patient.

"But my wife is also a nurse and she thinks she is dying," the husband said.

"No wheelchairs outside the ER," the supervisor repeated.

"The hell with that," the first line nurse said. "I'm going to try and save that patient!"

Policies, protocols and rules are important. But The Mother Test is not primarily about policies. It is the people, not the plans. Executing goals is such a complex task that the vision must be simple and clear.

PASSIONATE PROACTIVE LEADERSHIP VERSUS THE REACTIVE MEDICAL MODEL

The medical care model is reactive and that is how caregivers are trained. Emergency room doctors react to the patients that come through the door. Nurses in the Neonatal Intensive Care Unit react to newborns that may suddenly need help.

This is the way the medical treatment model is supposed to work. Doctors do not go door to door like salesman looking for customers. They are trained to treat the sick that come to them.

> *It is difficult to pioneer if you are spending all your time being a settler — and vice versa.*

This treatment model impacts leaders. CEOs can become defensive waiting for things to happen instead of passionate champions advancing a progressive agenda.

This may be one reason the hospital industry rarely produces breakthroughs. It is difficult to pioneer if you are spending all your time being a settler and being rewarded for keeping things calm.

Alexander the Great did not conquer the world by waiting for it to come to him. He drew on his inner energy and marched persistently out to win the day.

Thomas Edison expanded candlepower exponentially. He did not do it by lighting more candles. He persisted.

The British did not conquer a big part of the world by staying put on their small islands.

Steve Jobs did not create Apple to build more computers. His inspiring vision was to develop a whole new computer experience.

The Mayo Brothers did not found their now world-famous clinic by copying existing medical care models.

Both breakthrough pioneers and successful settlers work from the inside out. Their use of their inward strength supports bold and persistent action.

Laurie Harting prevails because she knows that outside forces shift and she must stay the course. Like the weather outside you cannot manage those forces.

Do not expect everyone to stand up and cheer. Resistance will surface immediately. It will continue so long as you are pushing the envelope.

When I came to Baptist Hospital in 1998 the old leader (who had been there for decades) was still around. In fact, he was elected Chairman.

Since finances were in a shambles, we all needed to develop a passionate commitment to turning things quickly. But the leader who I believed had led the organization into trouble was chair of the board to which I reported.

My side of the controversy goes like this: "Dan" the former CEO had led the organization into its $73 million dollar loss and he needed to step aside.

Ellen, the CNO at the time, told me, "Dan cannot be defeated. He's clever and tough. He's been here for decades. You just arrived. Don't challenge him. He'll kill you."

Doubt drew itself across the faces of my team. They had lived with what one of them called "fear tactics" and had watched others get fired. But the pioneering vision living inside me was powerful. I did not think it could be realized so long as Dan was Chair of the Board.

The short story is that after some very hard months of laying the groundwork I was finally able to convince the board to remove Dan. After that, the success story that became the new Baptist Hospital was launched and, just three years later, accomplished.

[After Dan left, I also suffered a life-threatening relapse in my Crohn's disease losing forty-seven pounds and, nearly, my life. The battle had taken its toll.]

No one wants to follow you if you just give orders. Intimidated staff members will follow orders. But fear will block the support, creativity and positive energy you need to pass The Mother Test.

> *The leaders you want will follow you if you inspire them with an exciting vision they want to realize, convince them the vision is achievable, and pioneer with them through the forest to success.*

UNDERSTANDING NITPICKING

Another challenge to passion is dealing with those who have trouble with big picture thinking. Join me at a medical staff meeting at Riverside Hospital in Toledo in 1977.

The staff gathered to hear the hospital's strategic plan. The first comment was from the Chief of Radiology. It was typical of other reactions from these people trained as physicians. "There are two typos on page fourteen and on the same page you referred to radiologic technologists as radiology technicians" he said.

I smiled. The doctors did not.

But what do you think of the *plan*?" I asked. The Chief of Staff interrupted, "I already see a lot of problems with your proposal so I suggest we table it."

Why would these bright physicians devolve immediately into nitpicking? Doctors are trained to diagnose trouble. Radiologists look for the spot on the X-Ray, not for the healthy tissue. His trained eye quickly caught typos instead of noticing the optimistic plans in the "healthier" part of the document.

> *Challenging a plan is fine. But nitpicking is for technicians, not leaders.*

There are five stages that lay the groundwork for change:

Stage One—Leadership

Culture change starts at the top. If the Captain of culture is not on board then the ship stays bound to the dock.

On the other hand, the moment the CEO embraces this work the organization moves. When Laurie Harting came on board in each of her new leadership roles she put her new ship on a better course.

That is why it is best if the CEO initiates change personally. The CEO is an admiral with many ships to guide. The Captains look to him or her.

At the Cleveland Clinic, the CEO appointed a physician, Dr. Bridgett Duffy, to lead the culture change. He named her Chief Experience Officer (CXO.)

As CXO, Dr. Duffy was empowered to guide the Clinic toward a stronger culture. Patient and employee satisfaction improved significantly enough so that Dr. Duffy's kind of role has spread to other organizations. The Clinic adopted our Servant's Heart training that has now spread to other hospitals.

Stage Two – Analysis of Current Culture

What markers matter?

❖ First, make a subjective judgment. Assuming you cannot intervene in any way, how confident would *you* be that everyone in your organization would treat your loved one as you wish?

❖ What is the dominant leadership style in your organization? Are leaders feared or trusted?

❖ What are patient satisfaction scores? How is employee morale? When patient satisfaction is low employee satisfaction is usually low also.

❖ What are current employee turnover levels? Above twenty percent turnover is typically a sign of cultural problems.

❖ How is the hospital viewed in the community? What is the quality of the medical staff? How is the physical environment? Do staff members have the resources and equipment they need?

Stage Three – Leader Alignment

Leaders are the first group that must be on board.

If your style is enlightened leadership you need colleagues who reflect that. If you have leaders that are fear drivers they need to be retrained or removed. Their style will defeat a model of enlightened leadership that values others.

Stage Four – Changing Interactions

Success in each interaction drives passage of The Mother Test.

Sometimes, the right people have not done well with some relationships because they have never received the right training. They may be unwittingly engaging in behaviors that are offensive rather than effective.

Stage Five—Changing Culture Drivers—The Goals

Culture changes when the drivers of culture are changed.

A relative of mine worked as a receptionist in a hospital for thirty years. Eve was a star associate and earned recognition as Employee of the Year.

Everyone loved Eve. Patients, visitors, fellow associates and doctors alike frequently complimented her on her exceptional work. Her supervisor felt otherwise. Gladys called my relative in for counseling.

"Eve, you are overdoing it," she told her. "You are leaving your post to guide people down the hallway. You are taking too long answering visitors questions. And you don't have to be cheerful all the time. Be professional!"

Eve was stunned. "I thought we were supposed to go the extra mile."

"Maybe," Gladys said. "But you are making my other employees look bad."

Great caregivers make average associates look bad. Weak employees are threatened by excellence and will try to destroy it. Loving care drives out mediocrity.

The Third Power
APPLYING POTENTIAL

If one advances confidently in the direction of his dreams and endeavors to live the life which he [or she] has imagined, he [or she] will meet with a success unexpected in common hours.

Henry David Thoreau

Although the seven powers have been listed separately they always work together. Part of purpose and passion involves assessing the potential of your team as a whole and your team members individually.

Churchill discovered that his small nation had the potential to defeat a much larger power. Gandhi initially assembled a small team to dislodge the British from centuries of British rule. Teresa began with only thirteen nuns. Roosevelt tapped all of his potential to lead our nation through Depression and World War.

Do not blame your team for failing to use their potential. It is up to you to build the right team and draw out their strengths and the best strengths in your organization.

That is what Jim Hinton did. He has spent his career developing the potential in people and in organizations. It was rough at the beginning.

In 1995, healthcare was on the precipice of significant change, and so was 36-year-old Jim Hinton. Jim was one of the youngest large-hospital CEOs in the country when he took the helm at New Mexico's Presbyterian Healthcare Services.

194

Presbyterian had just embarked on an ambitious move toward an integrated financing and delivery system by creating a health plan to complement the decades-old hospital network. Hinton saw potential—he saw an industry ready for change, he saw physicians and employees with the expertise and enthusiasm to adapt to a shifting landscape, and he saw himself as a leader who could bring the pieces together.

He was hopeful. He was curious. Instead of standing on the sidelines, he became one of America's Radical Loving Leaders by *changing* the game.

Today, Presbyterian Healthcare Services is New Mexico's only private, not-for-profit healthcare system with eight hospitals, a statewide health plan, and a multi-specialty medical group with more than 770 providers. While many hospitals that moved toward managed care in the 1990s eventually retreated from the integrated model, Presbyterian embraced the challenge and thrived doing it.

Jim credits Presbyterian's success to the more than 10,000 employees who are committed to a vitally important goal: Improving the health of their fellow New Mexicans. At Presbyterian, cultivating the potential of each employee connects directly to the organization's foundation and values.

"Understanding that *everyone* wants to be the best they can be is the key to unlocking human potential," says Hinton." Maybe one of our caregivers wasn't a superstar in high school but after we hire them we know they can be a star caregiver in our organization. That is our focus. To make sure every one of our staff is someone we would want taking care of our mother or other loved one. We have created an organizational setting that *cultivates potential.* Our culture promotes excellence and that is what our patients receive."

This is the kind of approach that lifted Jim Hinton to the chairmanship of the American Hospital Association. It is why he is one of our seven star healthcare leaders. It is why Presbyterian is an organization where the most capable and compassionate doctors and other caregivers want to work and where patients choose to come.

THE FIVE RELATIONSHIPS

The entire caregiving story turns on relationships. Meaningful work occurs through five encounters. Success or failure turns on the quality of those encounters.

Each day you engage numerous relationships. Here, you are invited to look through a new lens at how you and your staff encounter others and their *potential* to handle each kind of encounter more effectively.

Core encounters can be simplified into two categories: **Transactional** and **Meaningful** (or sacred.)

> *What if religion was each other?... If love was the center of our being.*
>
> Ganga White

A patient asks nurse Jan Shell for a glass of water and then says, "I am so frightened about my surgery tomorrow."

In a transaction, Jan ignores the patient's fear as "outside of her job description" but gets the glass of water. In a polite but incompetent transaction Jan says, "You have nothing to worry about" but forgets about the glass of water.

In order for an encounter to be truly meaningful Jan must bring her best self to the patient. That means she brings loving care. She makes sure to get the water but she also expresses compassion and reassurance.

Each encounter can be meaningful or simply a transaction.

The two kinds of encounters can be portrayed through a simple Venn Diagram. *A meaningful encounter occurs when Love meets need.*

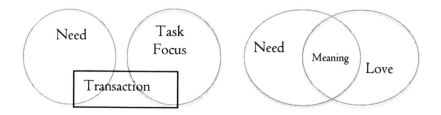

Cultures succeed when everyone uses their potential to make relationships work. Leadership, like budgeting, works through relationships, not spread sheets.

The Mother Test focuses on the five relationships you engage:

1. **Caregiver to Patient:** This is the reason you are here. You serve patients by *serving those who serve.*
2. **Caregiver to Caregiver:** Your relationship with your team members
3. **Caregiver to Leader:** The biggest determinant of employee satisfaction is how employees feel about their leader. Leaders impact organizational and team energy more than any other force.
4. **Caregiver to Environment:** How do you respect and honor your work environment and how do you ensure the work environment is supporting patient care and your employees. This includes workplace design as well as medical and computer equipment.
5. **Caregiver to Self:** The other five relationships can only work if you have learned to love, respect and care for yourself. How are you doing with self-care and self-compassion? Does your personal story nurture your leadership story?

Jim Hinton understands that radical loving leaders watch each relationship. He knows that every encounter can be meaningful, even sacred. Or it can be just a simple transaction.

You decide.

Your loving self, the self that brings your highest competence and your deepest compassion, is your best self.

Your fellow team member may only "need" a moment of your time. Bring your best self to that encounter. Your subconscious may interpret linoleum-clad paths lighted by florescence as depressing. Can you bring your best self to interpret this environment as part of a healing place?

1) Caregiver to Patient

Every hospital's mission is grounded in the first relationship. Hospitals were established so that patients in need could be cared for.

When two souls unite, whether for a few moments in a brief caregiving encounter or in a longer sacred relationship, can their love withstand winter's assault? Can they overcome the cold exhaustion that challenges love?

What does love expect of us? May Sarton offers a beautiful response: "Love… requires us to 'take in' the stranger and to understand him, and to exercise restraint and tolerance as well as imagination to make the relationship work." Caregivers need such a great measure of tolerance and imagination to meet the needs of the wide range of personalities they encounter. Only love can sustain.

Life and death created a sacred tableau between strangers at Baptist Hospital on December 18, 1999.

It was10:32 p.m. In half an hour, the day shift would depart. Soon the next shift would begin their journey across the dark hours and into dawn.

My leadership rounds concluded in the Neonatal Intensive Care Unit on the third floor. When I entered, Laura, a nurse was stroking the back of a tiny baby.

Over the decades, medical care for premature infants has gotten so good that babies who are less than two pounds are frequently saved.

> One life
> *But we're not the same*
> *We get to carry each other*
> *Carry each other.*
>
> "One" – Bono – U2

"How's the baby doing?" I asked cheerfully.

"He's dying right now," Laura said. "There's nothing else we can do."

"Where are his parents?"

"It was too much for them so they left. The baby will die with me," she said, continuing her gentle stroking of the baby's back.

There is nothing in the nursing manual or the rules of the Joint Commission on Accreditation of Hospitals that requires a nurse to stroke the back of a dying baby that has no chance of survival. Laura could have shifted to another infant who had a chance.

The dying baby, of course, could not ask to be accompanied in his final minutes. Nor could he thank the nurse for comforting him at his end. Ten minutes later he slipped the bonds of this earth.

The image of this caregiver and this patient are etched in my memory. There are millions of stories of patient care that happen every day. This one shines with an especially hallowed light.

2) Caregiver to Caregiver

We all love the story of the teamwork among geese. Wedging through the sky one will take the lead, the next pair forms a V and the next group begins to draft behind the first group. The further back in the V, the easier the flying.

Soon, the furthest back rotate until one of them is flying first against the headwinds. Thus, they fly hundreds of miles in perfect synchrony giving each other rest along the way.

Teams: The Currency of Compliments

In the eighth grade I got caught in a game that I now see demonstrated a powerful principle of negative team impact.

Early one school day classmates came to me and said, "When Bobbie comes in let's tell her she's not looking very good."

"But, we haven't even seen her yet," I answered naively.

"Are you going to play the game with us or not?" my peers challenged.

Buckling to the pressure, I was the first to confront Bobbie. "How are you doing," I asked.

"I feel great!" she answered enthusiastically.

"Well, you don't look too good. Are you feeling okay?"

Bobbie put her hand to her forehead as if taking her own temperature. "I think I'm fine."

Between 8 A.M. and noon five more kids told Bobbie she looked sick. At lunch, I asked where Bobbie was.

"She went home sick," a classmate told me.

Lest you think this is child's play consider the case of the great Yankee slugger Joe DiMaggio. Everyone knew that Joe was vain about his appearance. Just as DiMaggio was about to bat, a teammate said "Hey, Joe. You are lookin' good."

"Joltin' Joe" went out and hit a home run. After that, he asked the same colleague to always tell him he was "lookin' good" before he batted. Obviously, he did not stroke it over the fence every time. But he sensed the energy in a teammate's compliment.

Who decides how you feel? You may think that you make this decision. The truth is your actual energy often depends how your fellow caregivers treat you.

Affirmation awakens potential. Discouragement or indifference kill it.

That is why caregiver-to-caregiver support is such a big deal. Want to raise your team's energy? Tell your colleagues they are looking good. It does not matter if it is completely true. Thank them. Tell them you like having them on the team.

Mark Evans is the best Human Resources leader I ever worked with. We developed some of the finest partner and associate support programs any hospital ever developed. We had a world class day care center, grocery shopping on campus and a spectacular program of staff recognition.

We all want to be appreciated and affirmed. Compliment currency does not cost a dime. Yet, it can generate more energy for some caregivers than a pay raise.

3) Leader to Caregiver

The same compliment currency that works caregiver to caregiver is worth millions in the leader-to-caregiver relationship. The worst bosses scare their staff with actual and implied threats. The best ones offer sincere affirmation at every opportunity.

The attitude that leaders communicate to their staff about the quality of their organization can be crucial. Amazingly, many leaders can signal a lack of confidence in their own organizations. This negativity can be contagious. The reverse, of course, is equally contagious. Positive energy generates positive staff performance.

Ask your staff how they give loving care. Every time you do they get to teach you how they do it, and love increases.

The Problem with Wrong-Priority Leaders

Two years into running Riverside Methodist, Ohio's largest hospital, I set off to find which hospital was doing it best. It was 1985 and one of the premier names then, as it is today, was Massachusetts General Hospital.

Bob Buchanan, M.D. was the CEO back then and he granted me a one-hour interview in Boston. On the way to his office, everything looked typical to me. The staff who directed me to his office were abrupt and to the point. No one said "hello" to me in the hallways.

It was not until the last question that I finally learned something from Dr. Buchanan about excellence. My question was as direct and I could make it:

"Dr. Buchanan, if you needed to be hospitalized, where would you go?

"Well, I certainly wouldn't go here," he replied.

Seeing the stunned look on my face he followed up. "You have to understand, Erie. The priorities at "The General" go like this, he said, chopping the air with his hand: "Research, teaching, and then patient care." At the bottom of that air is where the patient landed.

"Where would you go?" I asked, still dumbfounded.

"Well, I wouldn't go here. I'd go to the BI (Boston's Beth Israel Hospital.) Mitch's (Dr. Mitch Rabkin) people take *great* care of patients. I think Mass General is the best hospital in the world. But the best hospital in Boston is The BI."

There it was. Instead of starting with *patient care as a top priority*, or at least ranking patient care equal with research and teaching, the boss of this world famous hospital confessed he would not choose the hospital he led.

I visited Beth Israel Hospital every year for the next ten years to learn why they were "the best in Boston." After all, they were a Harvard Research and teaching hospital like Mass General. Why was patient care so successful?

The answer came to me through my nominee for the best hospital CEO of the '80s and '90s—Dr. Mitch Rabkin.

Without offering detail here, I can summarize "The BI's" success in a few sentences. Dr. Rabkin not only placed patient satisfaction first but he led the creation of a culture of loving care unmatched in my experience. He did that in part through taking care of the people that take care of people, starting with his nursing staff, under the direction of Joyce Clifford.

Every new medical and surgical resident at Beth Israel either understood the culture shortly after their arrival or Mitch explained it to them: "Listen to the nurses," he told them. "Show them respect. If you don't you will not graduate from your training here."

One of the most interesting things about this approach is that it not only led to terrific employee and patient satisfaction but it spurred top clinical quality and successful financial performance.

That is how Jim Hinton brings out the best. He knows that enlightened leadership allows the garden of potential to bloom.

Today, if some hospital and system CEO's were honest, they would chop the air with these priorities: "Profits, safety, and then patient care." That is what I hear over and over again from first line caregivers. Many of them feel that their hospitals are engaged in "mission fraud."

---

4) Caregiver to Environment

One way you can appreciate the impact of environment is to take a vacation out of town. Changes in setting affect energy.

Environments impact health and healing. A man born in 1822 understood an aspect of this that affects all of our lives. He was Frederick

Law Olmsted and we owe to him the creation of landscape architecture. As just one example, what would Manhattan be like without his signature creation, Central Park? Those who visit there and even those who do not appreciate the impact of beautifully landscaped parks planted in cities. They bring us rest. They remind us of beauty. They are places to reflect and to play. They tell you the importance of your relationship with your environment.

Some caregivers try to warm the sterile settings of offices and nursing units and radiology suites by adding pictures of family or paintings of flowers. The best leaders engage architects to design employee and patient friendly settings.

Laurie Harting and her team built Mercy Gilbert Medical Center in Arizona from the desert up. They open up as much light as possible. They placed fountains and flowers wherever they could. They engaged the ideas of hundreds of staff along the way.

George Mikitarian did a similar thing at Parrish Medical Center. He brought his team on board, solicited their ideas and listened to his architects. The result is a gorgeous center that illuminates the lives of caregivers every day.

After battling with hospital bed-manufacturers, Tracy Wimberly, one of the finest and most loving leaders who every held an executive position, ensured that the beds in the maternity areas at both Riverside Methodist and Baptist had as much warm-looking wood as possible. Fountains were built into walls. Carpets were laid across linoleum to help new mothers (pregnancy is not an illness) feel at home.

Just as significantly, Tracy established a string of "pocket parks" around the campus at Riverside Methodist and a walking trail circled the hospital. Elevators were marked with fruit images instead of just numbers and poems were placed on plaques to be read while waiting.

Human Resources VP Mark Evans made sure that the new day care center on campus had a separate door sized so that little kids, and only little kids, could walk through on their own.

Ultimately, you decide how you relate to your environment. As a leader, look at the potential in the spaces caregivers use. Let them help you improve them.

5) Caregiver to Self

The winter morning lies still. Sun shines holly leaves. Up the hill, a cardinal red-dots the forearm of a little leaf oak.

Amid winter, a spring truth emerges: Only when you can love yourself can you love another. Therefore, start by imagining your beloved as you. Accept the power of self-care.

"The great malady of the twentieth century," Thomas Moore wrote in the 1990s, "implicated in all of our troubles and affecting us individually and socially, is 'loss of soul'."

Perhaps, you can see the proof of Moore's claim in your own life. When work is just a job it can steal your soul and leave you turning to addictions. Because your own life may seem unbearable, you may literally seek to escape it. Thus, self-care and a commitment to meaning is the only way to retain and nurture you spirit.

In the fifteenth century, Moore points out, Italians saw body and soul as united and thus the body was an expression of the soul. Modern thinking has split soul and body. Self care can heal this split. "When we relate to our bodies as having soul, we attend to their beauty, their poetry and their expressiveness."

First, we need to embrace the importance of self-care as essential to good other-care and to the quality of the way we live.

When my son was six months old he went on his first airplane. No one was listening as the flight attendant droned through the standard instructions about tray tables and seat adjustments.

Suddenly, she started into the part about how the oxygen masks would drop down if the plane lost altitude. My hearing sharpened.

Thinking ahead of her, I assumed what seemed obvious. Of course, you put the mask on your baby first.

Wrong. The mask goes on you first. You cannot help your baby if you are passed out.

Caregivers are terrible at giving themselves oxygen. This damages their ability to work at their full potential.

POURING GOLD INTO FLAWS

Nobody can hurt me without my permission.

Mahatma Gandhi

In the 15th century a Japanese shogun named Ashikaga Yoshimasa sent a cracked ceramic bowl to China for repairs. When it was returned, the cracks had been filled with disagreeable metal staples.

How else could the bowl have been repaired? the shogun wondered. A ritual was born.

The source of traditions in a country soaked with them can lead to entire philosophies. Over the past five hundred years the Japanese have converted the repair of cracked ceramics into the fascinating art of Kintsugi. Fissures are filled with gold.

Wabi-sabi is the gift of embracing flaws by making the crack *a place where beauty rises up from damage.* The marriage of wabi-sabi and Kintsugi births the art of self-healing, an invaluable analogy for you and your team.

Caregivers are forever berating themselves for not *being* perfect. We fill the cracks in our spirit with lead instead of healing them with gold. Kintsugi provides a loving metaphor through which we can acknowledge our imperfections with joy instead of self-loathing.

Love your flaws and then turn them into gold. Only love's gold can fill our "cracks" so that our lives bloom more beautiful than before.

Failures of self-care cause fatigue that leads to errors and burnout. The pressure of the immediate needs of others causes us to short-change ourselves. Meanwhile, some of us deny rest thinking we do not deserve it.

"It's a sad man, my friend, who's livin' in his own skin and can't stand the company," Bruce Springsteen sings. Are you often unhappy with who is inside your skin? Can you befriend yourself and become your own best companion?

We need to be kind to each other. We cannot do this unless we cultivate self-compassion.

On the other side of the world in the same century as Yoshimasa the sage Kahir offered encouragement:

Inside your body there are flowers.
One flower has a thousand petals.
That will do for a place to sit.

Sitting there you will have a glimpse of beauty
inside the body and out of it,
Before gardens and after gardens.

The seasons of your heart include spring mornings. At dawn, the brown earth yields to colors hidden for months. From the tips of winter-stripped branches green lace grows.

No need for you to brace yourself against a harsh wind today. Spring's breeze is soft as rose petals. Sit by the flower within you. Pour gold into your flaws.

One nurse I met insists on five minutes of quiet in her car before she starts her day and five minutes at home before she engages her family. In these five minutes she prays for both the competence to give good care *and* the compassion to embrace the treatment of disease—itself a "flaw." She knows she will be better afterwards.

It is such a good idea that it is hard to figure out why no one else does that.

You know your best self. You would spend more time there if it were not for all those outside forces that tire, irritate, bore and sometimes anger you. There's all that equipment that doesn't work right, the computer that runs slow and those aggravating people (including maybe your boss) that trouble your life.

What is the impact of caregiver anxiety on health? Husband and wife, the Doctors Glasser conducted a now-famous experiment on caregiver stress at The Ohio State University. They inflicted small circular wounds on the arms of two groups: high-intensity caregivers and non-caregivers.

Across several weeks they studied the speed with which the wounds recovered. It took nine times longer for the caregiver's wounds to heal than it did for the non-caregivers. But, caregivers do not need to quit their jobs to save their health. Several strategies can protect and advance caregiver health.

For example, physicians know that if you cultivate beauty, live love, exercise, eat well and find as little as five minutes twice a day to meditate and let go of worry your energy and effectiveness will improve exponentially. In fact, in his final days on this earth, as he suffered under the crushing weight of ALS, Bruce Kramer discovered that he *had* to have beauty for his life to be meaningful.

First, recognize how much caregivers and leaders need to practice a soft self-love amid the hard edges in hospitals. Gandhi entreats us to remember that, "There is more to life than increasing its speed." Pause now for just sixty seconds and close your eyes.

Recite three things you love about yourself. Is it your passion? Your purpose?

Compliment yourself for your ability to engage these energies.

Do this every morning and evening.

Once you accept that you not only need oxygen but also *deserve* it you will start taking better care of yourself. Be an example of self-care for your team. Encourage members to take vacations in their hearts as well as out of town by engaging

THE MAGIC 15 VACATION:

Five minutes of eyes-closed rest.

Five more to stretch.

Five more to gold-fill "your cracks" by reviewing what you love about yourself.

Each day, not unlike the patients you see, you leave the customized comfort of your home and the kindness of family and pets that love you for the hard-frame world of offices and hospitals populated by people many of whom are strangers to you. Make yourself your own best companion and carry that companionship everywhere you go. Infuse your life with self-kindness.

Give yourself the Magic Fifteen vacation every day. Watch your life improve. But, let's be real. It is unlikely that you will make this kind of change. So pick at least one of these five minute options. Even *one* minute with your eyes closed will help. Can you spare one minute to help your balance?

THE POTENTIAL TO CHANGE

"Circles of Influence"

Steven Covey's notion of Circles of Influence and Circles of Concern can help you figure out how to maximize the potential in your role. You may not be able to do much about a war in the Middle East or a drought in California but these may be in your Circle of Concern.

But Circles of Influence are regions in which you can use the energy in your potential to make a meaningful difference. By creating a culture of caring within your Circle of Influence you can affect the human experience of dozens or, depending on your role, even thousands of people.

In fact, you are exerting this influence right now. What effect are you having?

CAREGIVER TO PATIENT AND
LEADER TO CAREGIVER

Jan Shell is a nurse in a large Catholic Hospital. One evening, within her Circle of Influence, three call lights went on at once.

Jan's floor was short staffed. By the time she responded to the third call light twenty minutes had passed. She was anxious and exhausted. Her patient was angry.

"Where have you been?" the patient shouted. It took you so long I wet my bed!"

"Look," Jan said. "We're short staffed. You're not the only patient on this floor!"

Alan, Jan's charge nurse, overheard the exchange. Later, she told Jan two things: "I do not want you telling patients we are short staffed. Second, don't get angry at patients by telling them they are not the only ones on the floor. Cut that kind of talk out or I'm going to suspend you."

The next day another patient shouted at Jan for being late. Here is what she said, "I've been told not to tell you we are short staffed. But, the truth is we are."

Predictably, Alan's warnings backfired.

Jan once again scared her patient. After all, what can the trapped patient do about the hospital's short staffing? How does the fact of short staffing affect the patient's confidence in her care? How important does the sick patient feel when she is instructed she is not the only one with problems?

What else could Jan have said? How could Alan have led Jan more effectively?

In cultures of loving care, these questions answer themselves. Look at the potential to change the outcome in this key situation and every similar one.

In a compassionate exchange, Jan 1) apologies to the patient for being late, 2) empathizes with the pain the patient must have experienced while waiting and 3) tells her she is here now and wants to know how she can help.

In an effective leadership encounter Alan 1) expresses concern for the stress on Jan, 2) invites her to consider the impact of her statements, 3) invites her to consider other possibilities, and 4) supports suggestions that include the compassionate exchange option described above.

Stress and fatigue may *explain* unprofessional responses. In cultures of excellence they do not excuse irritation at patients.

LEADER TO CAREGIVER ENGAGEMENT OF RADICAL LOVING CARE

Jim Skogsbergh, President and CEO of Chicago's giant Advocate Health Care system, Lars Houmann, President and CEO of the superb Florida Hospital, Dr. Patrick Taylor, President and CEO at Holy Cross in Ft. Lauderdale and Dennis Swan, President and CEO of Lansing's excellent Sparrow Hospital, have been engaging the radical loving care approach for many years now. Through their leader-to-caregiver relationships they offer guidance on how to practice radical love to meet radical need.

Lead a culture of excellence where leaders honor others. Do not tolerate a culture of mediocrity in which caregivers demean others. Embrace excellence with all your heart, all of your mind and all of your soul.

The Fourth Power
APPLYING PERSISTENCE

God doesn't require us to succeed; He only requires that you try.

Mother Teresa

In the early 1970s a young student at Baylor felt that he heard God's call. In 1973 he heeded that call and took a position as an administrative assistant at Hendrick Hospital in Abilene, Texas under Boone Powell, Jr.

Today Joel Allison, a leader who followed his calling, is CEO at the 36,000-person Baylor Scott and White health system in Dallas. Joel says that, "faith, family and friends have been the inspiration and encouragement." That is what fueled his exceptional persistence over the past forty-three years.

Joel has two other key traits that characterize him as a radical loving leader. He is humble and he lives in gratitude. He has, "a sense of mission to be a servant leader and to make a contribution that hopefully makes life better for those patients and communities served..."

And Joel has always stayed grounded. "It is always about the people and building relationships that allow you to persevere and never lose sight of your calling and purpose in life," he says. "I have been truly blessed." And so have the people Joel leads and the patients they serve.

Why is Baylor Scott and White such a bright star in the galaxy of American healthcare? Watch how Joel Allison leads and you will see a big part of the reason.

213

DISCIPLINE AND FOCUS

Another example of persistence lives in what Carl Sandburg called "The City of Big Shoulders."

The Chicago area is home to a "Big Shoulders" leader named Jim Skogsbergh. Jim is President and CEO of the twelve-hospital Advocate Health System. Like Joel Allison, Jim started as an administrative resident after developing a deep interest in hospital leadership.

Because he runs a major health system with five billion dollars in revenues and 34,000 associates Jim has the chance to make a big impact on loving care in health care—and he does. After his election as Chair of the American Hospital Association he knew his influence as a radical loving leader would expand even further.

> *The country needs... bold, persistent experimentation.*
>
> Franklin D. Roosevelt, 1932

Since Advocate is a faith-based health care system loving care fits easily into mission. But, how does persistence figure into success?

"I believe there is a strong link," Jim says. "From my point of view keeping your eyes on the prize... requires discipline and persistence given all the other pressures and distractions that could pull you off course."

Jim knows that the hospitals he leads are there to deliver radical loving care not just ordinary care. He believes the mission has to be communicated in a "constant and consistent," way and that it is crucial to stay focused on "what's important and what and how we are trying to achieve our objectives."

Advocate Health System is a major success today because Jim Skogsbergh has kept his eye on the goal and made sure his leadership team does the same. If you are looking for examples of persistence in action, study Joel and Jim.

Persistence in Emergencies

It takes unusual persistence to deal with the endless challenges leaders face in the complex operation of hospitals. Emergencies are not always the ones that come to the door via ambulance.

One day in 2001 the electricity at Baptist Hospital failed. Then the back up generators malfunctioned. The lights went out in the Operating Room where surgeries were under way.

Patients, nurses and doctors called for help. It was time for professionalism, not panic. There is no room at such time for poor performers. Only the best staff working at their peak can deliver success in such emergencies. Fortunately, that is what happened.

Because our leaders had been persistently trained to be awake and alert, because we were already three years into our journey of excellence, we soon returned the hospital to full operations. When the lights went out, our team lit up their best energy.

Persistence and Routines

The vast majority of babies in most hospitals, including yours, will be born healthy. But if the staff has been allowed to "fall asleep" by mindless

215

repetition and robotic leadership, the baby can be strangled by his or her own umbilical cord. So can the organization you lead.

We are all at risk for falling into routines and failing to notice our own lives. How many sights on your way to work have you failed to see because you "drive that way every day?"

Joel Allison knows that consistent attention requires a persistent focus. He also understands persistence needs a rest and takes time each day to sit quietly and pray.

Loving leaders also appreciate that need for relaxation and variety. Work breaks are not "downtime" they are needed pauses to refresh the energy of first line caregivers.

SLEEPWALKERS

Ralph Ellison's words can be a wake up call for you and for all of us, "there are few things in the world as dangerous as sleepwalkers."

Are you surrounded by sleepwalkers? These are people who are working at ten percent of their capacity because they have learned how to get by on minimum effort. Good news. You have a huge opportunity. Look at all the unused potential living in many of your colleagues!

In a classroom or on a *training* vessel it is okay to have C and D students who may doze off. After all, they are in the learning stage.

In the real life world of an operating room or a sea battle there is no room for C and D students. The stakes are too high. These are matters of life and death, of victory or defeat, of failed treatment or surging recovery.

THE QUICK FIX VERSUS THE REAL FIX

Persistence can seem not only hard but also monotonous. Over the last couple of decades numerous leaders have looked at the success we wrought in several large organizations. Their impatience for quick results causes them to ask a self-defeating question: "What's your

> *The light that is hard won offers the greatest illumination.*
>
> John O'Donohue

trick, Erie?" Average leaders are always looking for tricks. They do not want to commit to the hard work that brings real change.

There is no trick. It is a process of culture change that takes a couple of years (in a large organization) to plant and many more years to grow."

Clunk. Who wants to do that? That is why the vision must inspire meaning. Without inspiration and perspiration you cannot make it to any new destination.

What is the best healthcare system in the country? As mentioned, some say it is The Mayo Clinic (although The Cleveland Clinic is becoming a stronger and stronger contender.)

How did The Mayo Clinic reach such exalted status? They put in place "The Mayo Way." Join that organization and you will quickly discover that you must perform to The Mayo Way or find work elsewhere.

The Mayo standard is so strong that leaders are not always the enforcers. Employees who notice an underperforming colleague have been known to say, "That is not the Mayo Way."

What is your organization's "Way?"

But "quick fix" leaders are never interested in these examples. "We're not the Mayo Clinic," they tell me, thus dodging the questions.

Who *are* they then? Are they a second rate organization not worthy of treating your mother? What can they do with what they have?

There are no examples I know of where "quick fix" leaders have brought about meaningful *positive* change. Quick staff cuts may make a difference in the bottom line. But as the old saying goes, you cannot cut your way to success. Only culture change that honors excellent staff has a long-term positive effect.

Although the sources of change require deep analysis and thought, they are not simple to list. To deal with our natural desire for steps, here are some followed by ways to succeed in climbing them.

ACTUAL STEPS TO ACTUAL SUCCESS

All great leaders adhere to these steps because they guarantee meaningful change. They look at the drivers of culture, hiring, orientation, training, promotions, rewards, terminations and so on. They change them to meet the new vision.

Average leaders give up fast. At a retreat with the executive team at one large hospital the team adopted a ten-point action plan. One of the easiest-to-implement points was the group's unanimous decision to make employees' nametags bigger to enable calling staff by their first names. A Vice President took responsibility to follow through.

One year later the name tag project to which every top leader agreed had still not been implemented. Most of the rest of the ten-point plan was also dead-on-arrival. While the leadership continues bickering with each other, the hospital is struggling to hold onto its average rankings.

Falling backwards financially, they ended up trying to cut all leadership pay by ten percent. After a negative reaction they bagged the plan after three months. Persistence has not characterized this leadership team.

Good news: every time leaders committed to implement every one of these tools the results have been spectacular.

HIRING – HIRE FOR A SERVANT'S HEART

Do not hire a man [sic] who does your work for money, but him who does it for love of it.

Henry David Thoreau

Hire the wrong crew in the wrong way and your ship will founder the moment storms arise. Successful companies like Southwest Airlines pay a lot of attention to whom and how they hire. Hundreds of hospitals pay remarkably little attention to this.

In one struggling hospital I discovered that the norm was to do "resume hiring." In nursing, for example, leaders were so desperate to fill some positions that they simply verified that the candidate had a current license and no criminal record and then offered the job.

One leader joked to me that she used the mirror test. "If I put a mirror under her nose and she fogs it up she's hired."

Use that kind of mirror test and you will never pass The Mother Test.

What is the right way? Hiring standards should reflect the core mission.

Hire for a Servant's Heart

Start adding new questions to the hiring and interview process. *Every* leader should always consider if the candidate has **A Servant's Heart**. Interestingly, good leaders always seem to know what that means.

Another great question is, "Tell me how you give loving care?" Remember, *everyone is a caregiver.*

If the candidate is an accounts receivable clerk ask them the difference between working at a hospital and working at a bank. If she cares about the caregiving mission of the hospital she will be more likely to be someone whose phone interactions support your vision.

ORIENTATION – WAKE IT UP!

It was ten o'clock in the morning when I was called upon to speak to fifty new employees at Baptist Hospital, Nashville's largest. I had been President and CEO for two weeks.

As I rose and turned to the audience I expected to see what I had seen so often at Riverside Methodist Hospital—a group of eager staff members in their first days at one of the best hospitals in the country. After all, eight years into my tenure at Riverside the Radical Loving Care strategy had worked so well that we had more than twelve applicants for every one job.

ABC NEWS had named Riverside one of the top ten most employee friendly hospitals in the country. Winning a spot on the Riverside staff was like making the Olympic team. Everyone wanted to look sharp.

Instead, at Baptist, I saw, with some exceptions, a group drugged into boredom. Half the audience was slouched down in their chairs. Three were dead asleep. One of those had his head tilted so far back it looked like he needed CPR.

What would you do with this group if you were their leader? I have asked different groups this question. One audience member said, "If I was the CEO I would wake those three up and fire them!"

Now, there is a fine solution. "Wake up you three. Welcome to Baptist Hospital where our mission is loving care for all. You're fired!"

I understand those who prefer the instant termination option. Who wants new employees that fall asleep on their first day? But firing them sends a sharp signal to everyone else. What kind of signal? Fear.

Fear is a powerful motivator, especially if you are an army sergeant who is about to send his platoon into a killing field.

But, a hospital is a place of love not war. The work of a nurse requires mindful caring, not mindless killing.

The presence of bored and sleeping employees signaled to me that our orientation process at Baptist was broken. Like farmers who have tilled the soil too many times we were simply copying the same ineffective system every other hospital was using.

Presenters were assuming their job was to dump as much information as possible onto their audience. They recited the pension and benefits programs, handed out lists of rules, and droned through Power Point slides with all the energy of a comatose patient.

The next day I extended an invitation to the Vice President of Human Resources to see what she could do to enliven orientation.

"What do you have in mind?" Ruth asked, using the classic reactive energy in which she had been trained by her previous boss.

"What I would like to see is what new employees would like to see: Presentations that are interesting, engaging and signal that they are now part of a great organization."

Ruth looked baffled. She had been in the job five years and no one had ever challenged her to be a pioneer. The previous CEO was someone she feared.

Two weeks later, she came back with her new plan. "We were thinking it would be good if we got new microphones, a new projector and a bigger screen since people say the Power Point slides are hard to read.

These were, of course, the recommendations of someone so terrorized by her previous boss that she was fearful of suggesting anything innovative.

PARTY TIME

"Ruth, find someone in your department who has a great sense of humor, someone who likes to party and who everyone thinks is kind of wild," I said." Ask her what she thinks an exciting orientation would look like."

If I had not been the CEO, Ruth would have told me I was crazy. Instead, she returned a week later with a colleague.

"Mr. Chapman, this is Barb," Ruth said. Then she pushed her chair back as if a firecracker was about to explode.

"Here's what I think," Barb said brightly. "What's fun? A party. Let's invite our new employee to a party, hang a disco ball from the ceiling in the auditorium, drape streamers all around and put up welcoming signs.

When the new employees come in I think they should hear Aretha Franklin singing RESPECT. That's for starters."

Ruth looked scared, as if I would fire Barb on the spot. She seemed to be physically moving her chair back so she could distance herself from Barb if I thought Barb's idea was as crazy as she did. Like Peter denying Jesus, it was almost like she was ready to say, "Barb, who's Barb? I don't know Barb."

Instead, I said, "Great! Terrific ideas. Let's get rolling."

"But this is a hospital?" Ruth said tentatively. "What if people think the party stuff is disrespectful."

"We need to do three things in orientation not just one," I said. "We need to inspire and entertain, not just inform. If we don't do all three than our orientation will continue to fail."

Baptist developed one of the best orientation programs in the country. The pension and benefits presentation was turned into games like "Family Feud" with teams competing against each other. Speakers were trained to convert their presentations into stories. Inspiration came from the process of inviting new employees to share with each other about why they entered health care.

We called this the IFF strategy (Information with Inspiration and Fun.) After that, new employees left orientation fired up and ready to go rather than bored and uninformed people starting just another job.

Use the IFF strategy in every presentation and in all of your work. Energy will rise and learning will increase.

NAVIGATORS

A superb follow-up to a great orientation is something George Mikitarian, one of America's finest hospital CEOs (at Florida's Parrish Medical Center) put in place several years ago. You should copy it. He recruited veteran associates to act as "Navigators" for new staff members.

New team members emerged from orientation with an associate who helped them find their way around. Imagine how good this made his new employees feel!

The navigator program signaled to staff right away that the hospital cared enough about them to support them in their new experience. A second benefit is that the navigators also felt empowered. As they guide their new partner they are able to teach and encourage, thus affirming the exact values the hospital is trying to teach.

TEAM TRAINING AND REARRANGING

One hospital I worked with recently was making excellent progress. Suddenly, they gave up on their latest leadership training thrust.

Why? A small group of leaders complained to the CEO that I was pushing them too hard and that I was not being "loving." [They seemed to have overlooked

> *Quick-fix leaders never lead meaningful change*

the "tough-minded" part of "tough-minded, tender-hearted" leadership.] The progress did not matter. They wanted a quicker fix that did not hurt so much. The CEO backed off. I am advised that progress has eased backwards.

Everyone says they can handle the tough stages before they actually face them. Most people turn back somewhere along the voyage and never become their best selves. And every leader needs to know how to help his team have fun here and there along the way. Singing was an integral part of The Civil Rights movement!

Your new associates have now experienced a rigorous hiring process and an encouraging orientation. They also should have a navigator, typically from another department. If you've hired for a Servant's Heart and offered an inspiring orientation they are now fired up to start sailing.

COACHES

This is one of those common sense steps that is rarely practiced. Everyone should be coaching and mentoring someone. Remember that a key to success with your learning is that you pick a partner and be a learner as well as a teacher. This nurtures your own excellence, the success of the other, and the culture of loving care you seek. That nurtures cultures of excellence.

Leadership coaches are also crucial to helping leaders learn skills they may never have considered or practiced. Liz Viera does that work brilliantly at Parrish Medical Center

Leaders can also establish specific partnerships in the organization, preferably from people who do not work in the same department. In each monthly meeting each partner does two things: 1) Asks the other how they are doing and 2) Teaches the other partner what they have learned and practiced.

Big time sports teams have layers of coaches. Some football teams not only have offensive and defensive coaches but they also have line coaches, quarterback coaches, linebacker coaches, special team coaches, strength coaches and more. Note that each of these key leaders is called a *coach*. Their goal is not only to design plays and give directions. It is to improve and enhance the performance of their team and each member of it.

THE ENORMOUS IMPACT OF PEER PRESSURE

> *The single biggest drag on performance is bad peer pressure. The best driver of peak performance is a top quality team.*

Remember your first day of school or your first day on a new job? You checked peer behavior. You watched and learned to comply or leave. Now you can change the culture to support positive peer pressure.

What if your new associates join a crew that is flat, a team that is riddled with folks that are not passing the mother test? Imagine them entering that new department.

An associate takes them aside and says, "Watch out for the boss. She is a tyrant. Just keep your head down and follow the rules."

What if they are an electrician working in HVAC and see a bunch of colleagues working at ten percent of their potential? What if they are a physical therapist and find their team is discouraged and disheartened and led by a cynic who cares only about meeting budget?

The single biggest support for a loving culture is positive peer pressure. The single biggest killer of performance is bad peer pressure. A top quality team naturally pressures everyone to perform at their best.

It is your job as a leader to see that your team is strong. Trim out the weak performers and train to evoke talent, reward the best, and affirm the team as a whole.

All of this is simple to say and hard to do. That is why leading on this new voyage requires coaching! Train and coach your team using The Mother Test.

Tell stories. For example, an electrician was called to repair wiring in a patient room at Baptist Hospital. After the job was complete, the patient said, "Thank you. You are a great electrician." The electrician said, "I'm not an electrician, I'm a caregiver. Good wiring supports good patient care."

The identical thing was true with Lois Powers. Lois was a long-term associate who worked as a cashier in the cafeteria. One day I studied the four checkout lines and noticed that almost everyone coming through Lois' line left smiling.

"Why does everyone leave your cash register looking happy," I asked.

"I tell a new joke every day," she told me. "Not everyone thinks it's funny but everyone smiles anyway."

"What do you do if the person looks sad?"

"I know they may have experienced a death. If I see sadness I don't tell the joke. I just touch their arm and smile."

"Wow, you are a great cashier," I told Lois.

"I'm not a cashier, Mr. Chapman, I'm a caregiver."

Joel Allison persists in trimming out or retraining the staff members that he sees are pulling down team performance. His guideline is that an ideal staff member is both tough-minded and tender-hearted, both competent and compassionate.

Joel appreciates that every employee and leader is a caregiver, not just nurses and therapists and doctors.

Place your team members in one of three groups: C) Weak performers who will never make it B) Average performers that can be trained to become peak performers, A) Peak performers that regularly pass The Mother Test.

Remove, retrain, reward. Remove the C group (you do not want them caring for your mother.) Retrain the B group. Reward the A group.

Above all, follow Joel Allison's example. As a radical loving leader Joel is a model of humility. That comes from his deep faith. He knows that God is love. That is the kind of partnership he has always engaged. It has helped him be persistent.

Teaching Tool: The Mother Test Window

Competent (Fire Driven) AND Compassionate (Light Filled) **Leader Action**: Recognize, Reward & Highlight. These are the people I want caring for mom.	Competent, NOT Compassionate **Leader Action**: Review & Refer for Training so they can pass The Mother Test
Compassionate, NOT Competent **Leader Action**: Review & Refer For Training so they can pass The Mother Test	NOT Competent NOT Compassionate **Leader Action**: Likely termination. (I don't want them dealing with my mother.)

The Fifth Power
APPLYING POSITIVITY

I can do things you cannot, you can do things I cannot; together we can do great things.

Mother Teresa

PROFILE OF POSITIVITY

If there is a health care utopia in America it may well be in the small city of Rochester, Minnesota. I ask health care professionals all the time where they would go for a rare and complex medical problem if they could not come to their own hospital. Time and again, I hear the same answer: the Mayo Clinic.

Since 2009, the great leadership legacy of Mayo has been in the hands of one of Dr. John Noseworthy. He has proved himself to be one of America's finest radical loving leaders. He is also a profile in positivity.

John knows the kind of reputation Mayo has. When then-President Ronald Reagan injured his head in a fall from his horse in 1989 you would have thought he would have pursued treatment at one of California's fine hospitals. Instead, he boarded a private jet and flew halfway across the country for care to the Mayo Clinic.

What do physicians think? After nine years practicing at Mayo, world-class pediatric neurologist Marc Patterson took an opportunity to be chief of pediatric neurology at the well-regarded New York-Presbyterian Hospital. Within a year, he was back. "At Mayo the focus is on the patient. The needs of the patient come first," Dr. Patterson said in a 2002 interview for *Health Beat.*

Why is the Mayo Clinic so often cited as the gold standard in healthcare? Obviously, superb quality and breakthrough research stand tall. But, the biggest reason seems to be *the clear focus on patient needs.*

Dr. Noseworthy agrees with this. He is often asked what sets Mayo apart. Many assume he will emphasize superb quality or breakthrough research. Instead, he says, "We feel our people, and their approach to patient care, distinguish the Mayo Clinic."

Even in an interview with a business newspaper he focused on people instead of money: "Investing the time, energy, and resources in our staff, and demonstrating to them what needs to happen, then *letting their creativity go* and harnessing that going forward is unquestionably our best investment,"

The performance of John's thousands of caregivers reinforces that he has put the focus in the right place. Few physicians and nurses and therapists are more dedicated to their organization then those that work for Mayo.

Radical Loving Leaders like Dr. Noseworthy signal their values through their positive stories. "[B]efore I worked here, one experience told me all I needed to know about Mayo's mission and its staff," he writes. "As a young physician, I was asked to host a dinner for an internationally recognized Mayo neurologist who was coming to the university where I was working to accept a prestigious award. The physician missed the dinner appointment. He apologized later, saying he'd missed his flight because he was with a patient. I knew then that at Mayo the patient is always first, and I wanted to devote myself and my life's work to such an institution."

There are many metrics that signal a team's success. The typical ones include clinical quality, research success, budget targets, team morale, staff turnover, employee satisfaction (the biggest determinate of employee satisfaction is not the job. It is how they feel about *you*) and organizational reputation.

Reputation? People at Mayo love to tell others where they work. No large organization consistently gains such superb reviews from patients.

But, there is another thing people like Dr. John Noseworthy understand well: The numbers do not always answer the problems. The key ends up being subjective. It is *leadership judgment.* This means looking beyond metrics to evaluate what you believe to be true.

A POSITIVE PICTURE OF LOVING LEADERSHIP

Based on a May 11, 2015 report in Becker's Hospital Review (a superb resource for healthcare leaders) one of the finest Radical Loving Leaders in healthcare appears to be Chris Van Gorder, president and CEO of San Diego's Scripps Health. Like Randy Oostra, CEO of ProMedica, Van Gorder has reached beyond Scripps' immediate service area to offer staff to help earthquake victims in Nepal.

Back at home Van Gorder is emerging as a loving leader who practices what he preaches. On a regular basis he rounds with first line staff and also conducts question and answer session with employees. The heart of Chris's loving leadership lies in this key quote: "...what's the most important thing we do?" he asks. "It's at the front line, where we deliver healthcare."

Chris Van Gorder gets it. Following every tenet described in this work, he emphasizes stories. In every gathering of his 600 leaders, stories are told about *patients*. Chris worries that "...as we talk about the complexity of the business, the patient gets lost in the equation." He knows a way to counter this. "Firsthand accounts of healthcare delivery—from patients themselves—serve as a powerful reminder of employees' mission and purpose."

This kind of leadership has led hospitals in the Scripps system to top-twenty performance nationally in several key categories. Congratulations to Chris and his team for understanding why Radical Loving Leadership is the right path for patients, caregivers and their leaders."

CHALLENGES TO POSITIVITY—TERMINATIONS

The Impact of Incompetent and Inconsiderate Caregivers

> *One love*
> *One blood*
> *One life*
> *You got to do what you should.*
>
> "One" – U2, Bono

Leaders like Mayo's Dr. Noseworthy have learned to make the tough decisions. John knows that removing poor caregivers is not cruel. It is an act of love because the stakes are high in hospitals. Every day, errors can bring injury or death.

So, the "cruelty" is not in firing a subpar caregiver. It is in continuing to employ a caregiver who is creating bad patient experiences.

Healthcare is serious business. John's standards require genuine compassion as well as top competence in the organization he leads.

Incompetence can result in malpractice. Lack of compassion can ruin a patient's emotional experience and can damage treatment and recovery.

The awful truth is that thousands of healthcare leaders delay terminations that are clearly indicated. They know who their weak performers are. Some have been there for years, even decades. Some are tough but lack compassion. Some are compassionate but lack competence. Some are simply chronic underperformers in both categories.

I have heard leaders recite every excuse possible for why they cannot terminate Judy or Bob. You can overcome every one of these excuses by applying The Mother Test.

Here are some of the common excuses:

1) **Pity:** "I cannot let Judy go. She is the sole support for her family." Or, "Sally has cancer."

This is tough, of course. Always remember the key question: Do you want Judy or Sally taking care of your mother. If not, then make a change on factual grounds and leadership judgment, not personal dislike.

2) **Long Term Staff:** "Bob has been here forever."

If Bob is an underperformer this means he has been doing this year after year. His time is up.

3) **Satisfactory Reviews:** "Sharnel has always had okay reviews."

It is time for *you* to raise the standards. Start giving Sharnel the reviews she deserves. Give her a three to six month chance to meet the standards.

4) **Popularity:** "Everyone likes Maria. If I fire her the team will revolt against me."

You are not in a popularity contest. When you act, act firmly. Share the news with the rest of the staff in a respectful way. Tell them you understand they like Maria but the key is patient care, not popularity. Let them get mad at you. They will move past Maria sooner than you think. You have signaled that you only want the best staff.

RADAR DODGERS

When I joined Riverside in Toledo there was a vice president who had been there for fifteen years. He was responsible for physical therapy, the lab and several ancillary service areas. Bud rarely left his office.

"I like to keep my head down," Bud told me. "That is how I've survived all these years. My team does okay. I don't want to attract attention. That's how I keep my job."

Bud refused to change in a changing environment. In other words, he was not willing or able to accept become a tough-minded tender-hearted leader. When I became CEO eighteen months later I let Bud go. "Why are you doing this to me?" he asked. "I did okay, didn't I?"

"Yes, you did," I told him. 'Okay' is not good enough for patients or your staff. We need excellence."

Bud had tried to straddle the dock and the boat for too long.

The "Radar Dodgers" are fascinating. They are in a class by themselves. They have been around forever. They are underperformers but they have one spectacular skill, dodging the radar.

Whenever there are layoffs or terminations these employees somehow vanish from the screen. I do not know how they do it.

Every organization has Radar Dodgers. Because they will slow you down on your journey to excellence you must root them out and move them out.

ENERGY THIEVES

The ideas are flowing in the ten-person meeting. The discussion is flooded with new hope. Ten faces shine with expectation.

Suddenly Jake walks into the room. He has not said anything yet but you can feel the hope shrinking and the muscles tensing.

Finally, Jake speaks. "What are we wasting our time on today?" he says. If everyone were wearing the medical monitors used for heart patients you would see the numbers making troubling turns.

Jake is an energy thief.

It is remarkable how much energy a thief like Jake can pilfer. Across an eight-hour day or a twelve-hour shift productivity is down when he is there and up when he is out of town.

Wondering why some of your performance scores are stuck? Beware of the energy thieves. The day you move them out you will see performance rise along with your chances of passing The Mother Test.

CHAMELEONS

You know these folks. They tell you what you want to hear but, behind your back, they change colors and turn on you.

Sometimes this is because they do not feel safe offering suggestions or criticism. As a result, you contribute to their color-changing behavior.

Remember why chameleons change their colors. It is for protection.

THE TEETER TOTTER PRINCIPLE AND THE MOBILE

You know how they work: If someone is down and you want to lift them up, climb on the empty seat of a teeter-totter. If you want to hurt them, suddenly jump off of your end.

Watch the perfect alignment of a mobile at rest. Tap just one piece of a mobile and watch *all* the other pieces move. When a person gets cancer, it disturbs not only his balance but also that of every single person close to him.

The simple physics of the teeter-totters and mobiles reflect the role of balance in organizational psychology. Every leader has the power to apply his or her "weight" to lift up a colleague or to hurt their energy. Every time a leader fires a team member it affects the balance of every member of the team not just the one who has been terminated.

DIFFICULT CONVERSATIONS

First, keep in mind that your job is ensure best care for patients and caregivers. Average work is dangerous in caregiving organizations.

No patient says, "Please put me on the floor with one of your average teams. No one says, "I'd like one of your least successful surgeons." No accountant says, I want to work for a Chief Financial Officer who will treat me badly.

If the clerk who just sold you a shirt puts the wrong one in the bag you can return it. But if a doctor removes the wrong leg in surgery you cannot grow it back.

Successful executives study human behavior. If you keep below average performers on board you will show yourself to be a hypocrite and sap energy from your best staff.

If your termination decision is because of bad chemistry be honest. "Ed, this is not about performance. The difficulty is that you and I do not work well together. I take full responsibility for that." This approach is honest and it works.

When the termination is because of poor performance I have said exactly that: "Sally, you are a fine person but *the record shows* that you have shown poor judgment too often."

When the employee challenged me I would often say, "Maybe you are right and I am making a mistake. But, I believe it is the right thing to do."

The human resources department will make sure you are following the law and appropriate policies. The goal here is to help you enter these difficult conversations with confidence rather than with indecision.

On rare occasions, I have terminated staff members for outright wrong-doing or inappropriate behavior. I have been much tougher in these situations.

LAYOFFS

The fundamental difference between terminations and layoffs is that terminations are *for cause* and layoffs are not. Layoffs happen because money is short or the job is no longer needed.

When you lay people off consider the following guidelines:

❖ Do *not* dismiss the employee and have security escort them to their car unless they are clearly dangerous. *Do* honor and affirm the person before you.

❖ Do *not* blame the employee. This is a layoff, not a termination. *Do* take full responsibility.

❖ Do *not* tell the person "this is nothing personal." It will feel personal to them. *Do* tell them how much you regret having to take this action.

❖ Do *not* tell them you understand how they feel. *Do* tell them "I cannot imagine how hard this must be for you."

This is a classic opportunity for the tough-minded tender-hearted approach. You need to be firm and take responsibility. You also need to be kind and compassionate.

One reason Dr. John Noseworthy is so successful is that he uses *the magic of positivity* to breed hope and high energy.

All great leaders engage the unseen powers of love and hopeful thinking. That is how they awaken exceptional power. That is part of what happens through a clear and compelling vision, the kind of thing you can do in your life and work.

> *Heaven goes by favor.*
> *If it went by merit,*
> *You would stay out*
> *And your dog would go in.*
>
> Mark Twain

To communicate confidence John clearly uses inner powers to create outside energy. Because doctors are trained to diagnosis illness hospitals are often flooded with pessimists. A leader does not have the luxury to indulge in pessimism. But, he or she must also tell the truth, and frame it as positively as possible.

BUTTERFLIES

How can one leader, or one individual, alter the lives of many others with simple positive acts? Caroline Myss writes that, "There is no such thing as a simple act of compassion or an inconsequential act of service. Everything we do for another person has infinite consequences."

One morning, Chris Rosati guided his wheelchair into a restaurant and maneuvered over to a table where two girls, age 13 and 10 were sitting. He handed each a fifty-dollar bill. "Do something kind" he said. "It's up to you."

Three months later, Chris opened his email. There was a photograph of a group in Sierra Leone holding up a sign. "Thanks a lot for spreading kindness, Chris," the sign said. The money had helped these impoverished people have a feast.

The girls in the restaurant had done "something kind" with their fifty-dollar bills. When interviewed on CBS they sounded joyful and grateful. The people in faraway Sierra Leone also looked joyful and grateful. Chris Rosati is also joyful and grateful, even though ALS is stealing more of his body every day.

Chris is enchanted by something scientists call "The Butterfly Effect," a notion that says that a single butterfly flapping his wings in one part of the world can cause high winds thousands of miles away. The theory may sound far-fetched, as unlikely as Chris handing out a pair of fifties to two strangers who end up hosting a feast for people in Africa.

One of Abraham Lincoln's lovely observations was that, "Most folks are as happy as they make up their minds to be." We can be as optimistic as we want to be.

Part of the problem is that too many pessimists think that optimism is a bunch of unrealistic, smile-all-the-time nonsense. Instead, it is the strategy by which all fine leaders succeed.

One key John Noseworthy understands about radical loving leadership is something Bobby Kennedy said years ago, "Take your work seriously not yourself." John also knows that loving care breeds success in improved clinical quality and financial performance, not just in patient and employee satisfaction.

THE IMPACT OF POSITIVITY

As Richard Rohr wrote: "When you start positive, instead of with a problem, there is a much greater likelihood you will move forward positively too."

Dr. Noseworthy, of course, knows that positivity is not simply a surface strategy of smiles and Hallmark card slogans. Effective positive thinking runs deep at The Mayo Clinic. Leaders there appreciate that well-framed optimism promotes healing.

Positive energy inspires positive energy. This truth is reinforced every day through the success of countless organizations, football teams, politicians and artists.

"CAMELOT"

For the three years starting in 1983 Riverside Methodist Hospital patient satisfaction rose from the 68th percentile to the 98th percentile. It remained in that range year after year.

Bottom line performance went from $2 million dollars per year to $20 million and ultimately $56 million in FY'95 for an OhioHealth system in which Riverside was the flagship.

Clinical performance improved dramatically as Centers of Excellence were established in Heart, Cancer and Women's Health. The Chairman who took over after I left ultimately referred to 1983-1995 as "The Camelot years."

Under the leadership of Dave Blom, someone I hired years ago, OhioHealth continues to thrive and financial performance is even stronger.

These are the kind of concrete results hospitals need and patients demand. These are the kind of outcomes you can help deliver.

Leaders like Dr. John Noseworthy, Laurie Harting and Joel Allison are often at their best when they are inspiring others and also helping them have fun. They understand the impact on others of the tone they set. They know how to season professionalism with humor.

Hospitals are grim places. No one wants to come to them and everyone wants to leave. No one says on a Saturday night, "Where shall we go for fun? Let's go check into a hospital." But, it is possible to joke in the middle of tense times. And it is possible to inspire amid crises.

After President Ronald Reagan was shot, a terrified Nancy Reagan asked her husband at the hospital how he was doing.

> *There's very little advice in men's magazines, because men don't think there's a lot they don't know. Women do. Women want to learn. Men think, 'I know what I'm doing, just show me somebody naked.'*
>
> Jerry Seinfeld

"Honey," Reagan said. "I forgot to duck."

When this joke was reported on the news the country took a collective sigh of relief. If the President could joke after being shot then the country was in good hands.

Have as much fun with your team as you can. It is great for energy. Hold parties to celebrate team performance.

Dr. Patrick Taylor, CEO at Holy Cross Hospital, tells jokes like these at meetings: "I'm reading a book about gravity. I can't put it down." Or, "PMS jokes aren't funny. Period." Or "The Energizer Bunny was arrested. He was charged with battery."...or "I didn't like my beard at first. Then it grew on me." ... "I stayed up all night to see where the sun went. Then it dawned on me."

He knows these are silly. All puns are. But, a team that is laughing together is not quarreling. Energy goes up. Stress goes down.

REWARDING, CELEBRATING
AND AFFIRMING YOUR STARS

A friend loves to repeat this line from Oprah Winfrey, "The more we celebrate life the more there is in life to celebrate."

If terminations are the hardest part of your job then affirmations should be the most joyful. Positive leaders reward stars. That does not just mean handing out bonuses and plaques. The most effective leaders I know are geniuses at affirmation.

Catch your staff being good instead of constantly punishing them for mistakes. The more you celebrate success the more success there is to celebrate.

ROUNDING

Rounding was established by doctors as a word to describe a process. Doctors would go *around* the floors checking up on patients. Leaders adopted this practice as a way to check on staff, to ensure that everyone was present, charts were done and work was proceeding as planned.

But, the better a leader is doing the less he or she needs to "check up" on his fellow adults. Instead, rounding provides one of the single best ways to spread energy through affirmation.

You do not need a four-alarm smile to be good at rounding. What we all need is an ability to be present and to demonstrate caring and support. Good rounding can be more about teaching experience. Let the staff teach *you* about their work.

An incredibly valuable rounding practice is to work one shift a month with first line staff in a different part of the hospital or hospice. One afternoon, I accompanied nurses during a delivery, what seemed sure to be a positive experience.

After the birth, the new mother called her mom. "It's a girl!" she told her with all the energy she could muster after a hard delivery.

"I said, it's a girl," she repeated.

Suddenly, the new mother's face fell. "Well, I'm *sorry* Mom. It's a girl." The old mom managed to kill the enthusiasm of the new one.

In the hallway afterwards, Gloria, a veteran housekeeper walked up smiling. "Want to see what I do every day?" she asked.

> *Not all of us can do great things. But we can do small things with great love.*
>
> Mother Teresa

"Sure," I answered.

"Well, you probably *don't* want to see," she said, gesturing to the vacant delivery room. Gloria's assignment was to clean up the blood and the afterbirth. Wonder who truly does the "dirty work?" Think about Gloria. Thank all the "Glorias" you can find.

Leaders do not have the luxury of ignoring rounding. In one case at a mid-size hospital in Toledo, a Vice President frustrated with the poor way Fred, his boss, rounded gave him the book, *Management By Walking Around.*

The VP told me, "Fred literally walked up one hall and down the other. Along the way he gave perfunctory nods to staff. His trip around the hospital took ten minutes. At the end, he said to me, "Well, I walked around like the book said."

In the second case, the CEO, a reserve Navy officer, maintained such a military demeanor that he scared the daylights out of everyone he visited.

The third case of rounding failure was the hardest.

"Ralph," is a physician CEO with a brilliant engineering mind and spotless integrity. He was trained as a doctor, not a leader. When I met him he was poor at rounding (also, his staff quarreled often in ways that damaged the organization.)

After repeated coaching, Ralph improved a little. He put away his cell phone when he walked the halls, spoke to people by name and asked about their families. He responded to encouragement to tell jokes. I even suggested one: "I'm so shy that my pet is a Hermit Crab." He should have used it. Self-deprecating humor is the best.

To Ralph's great credit, he tried. But this CEO had trouble saying hello to the staff in the C-suite. He walked by secretaries each day and into his office. He even refused to visit the VP in the office right next to his. One day, this VP shared with the CEO that she would be out for three weeks for serious surgery. "He never once expressed any good wishes or prayers," she said to me bitterly. "After I returned, he never once asked me how I was doing, no cards, no comments, no flowers, no notes... nothing."

Weak rounding is rampant in America. Visit the Kroger store where I sometimes shop. The manager cares nothing about the stories his check-out clerks tell. Every time I go through the line the clerks discuss how soon their shift is over, when they will get their lunch break or how happy they are that it is Friday.

Last time I asked a Kroger clerk where the cashews were he said, "I don't know, I work in produce. Anyway, *they've* moved everything around." (At a well-run store, the clerk would say "we" not "they.")

"That doesn't seem like very good customer service," I persisted.

"You're right," he said. "I hate working here. They treat you like you're a robot."

> *The difference between the right word and the almost right word is the difference between lightning and a lightning bug.*
>
> Mark Twain

At Whole Foods the associates tell different stories. They love talking to customers. Whenever I ask a Whole Foods employee how they like working there they always say, "I love it." They do not say they *like* it. They say they *love* it.

The employees at Southwest Airlines use the same language. They are the happiest and most upbeat employees I encounter in my travels. That alone would be enough. But it turns out that they, and their airline, do a fantastic job flying planes safely, on time and with rare lost luggage. Their profitability has been consistently strong.

Last time I asked an American Airlines flight attendant how she liked her work she said, "It used to be a lot better seven or eight years ago. Now it's a drag."

You can script employees to say certain things. But you cannot script sincerity and positivity. You do this by example and encouragement.

PUBLIC SPEAKING

It looked to me like it was going to be another boring half-hour speech at that Columbus Rotary meeting on a Monday in 1991. Programs were often so uninspiring that audience members dozed off within minutes. I used to watch their eyelids go down like garage doors one at a time.

This speech was different.

The speaker was American success story, Dave Thomas, founder of the giant Wendy's chain. The long introduction recited Thomas's grand accomplishments and how he had not graduated from high school. Thomas rose and gave one of the most memorable speeches I have ever heard: "I've had a lot of success in the hamburger bidness." (He always said the word like that.) Questions?"

The speech was over in less than five seconds. The garage doors had not even begun to go down among the crowd of three hundred. I loved this speech because Thomas delivered his one-line truth with humility and

246

clarity. We all knew his life story. His message was that he worked hard on one idea and rang the bell.

We remember 10% of what we hear, 20% of what we read, 70% of what we do and 90% of what we teach.

Talk less. Use humor. Always frame ideas in the positive. Create settings where team members teach each other.

Watch the example of Dr. John Noseworthy at Mayo Clinic. Notice that underneath his positivity is humility. That is what enables him to recognize that he cannot do it all by himself. He needs a team of positive partners to succeed.

The Sixth Power
APPLYING PRESENCE

PROFILE IN PRESENCE

He suffered from dyslexia before the affliction had a name. But, he wanted to be, of all things, a physician and surgeon. How could he ever accomplish such a big thing when dyslexia is such a big obstacle to learning?

But he won top grades in college. His perseverance enabled him to succeed once again in medical school. As his medical career progressed he found himself caring for wounded soldiers as a flight surgeon in Viet Nam. He won the Bronze Star.

There are many fine physician leaders. But, most doctors are not automatically effective as leaders. It is not how they were trained.

Delos "Toby" Cosgrove, M.D. is the exception. He is the picture of a doctor who has become a leadership virtuoso. President and CEO of The Cleveland Clinic, another great mecca for patients worldwide, Dr. Cosgrove has, for several years, put improving the patient experience at the top of his agenda. He was one of the first to appoint a Chief Experience Officer, Dr. Bridget Duffy, to assist him in overseeing major improvements at The Clinic and together they laid the foundation for the better experiences patients have today.

Dr. Duffy, in turn, engaged the teaching of Radical Loving Care and other concepts to help The Clinic focus on *servant leadership*. Together, they revolutionized the entire human experience as they developed "The Cleveland Clinic Way."

What kind of insight does it take for one of the top medical centers in the world to engage Radical Loving Care? "Patients... may not understand the technical know-how that a doctor must have in order to perform a complex heart surgery or neurosurgery, but they can form clear judgments about their experience," Dr. Cosgrove says.

He recognizes that suffering is more than medical pain. "Patients know whether their rooms are clean and whether people are polite to them. They recognize differences in the quality of the food and in how an organization looks and feels. They know whether they feel cared for. *Most of all, they can tell whether they've had a healing experience—or whether being in a hospital has only impeded their healing.*"

It is not easy for a tough-minded heart surgeon to engage the language of healing beyond curing. That is why Dr. Cosgrove is so clearly a radical loving leader. Meanwhile, he has continuously excelled in competence as well as compassion. *U.S. News and World Report has ranked* The Cleveland Clinic number one in cardiac care from 1994 up to the latest ranking available—2014.

PROFILE OF A HEALING HOSPITAL CHAMPION

He was selected as America's Healing Hospital CEO of the Year a few years back. Look closer and you will see why. In forty years, Jason Barker is one of the finest leaders I have met. Like Toby Cosgrove, George

Mikitarian, Laurie Harting, and each of the other radical loving leaders, Jason puts people first. As a former CFO, he has never been guilty of being "penny-wise and *people* foolish."

His record running hospitals from California to Montana is a story of converting cultures from ordinary to excellent. For example, his leadership transformed St. Vincent Hospital in Billings, Montana from the market follower to the market leader in less than two years.

Jason is a teacher. Like Dennis Swann, President and CEO of Sparrow Health System, Jason uses *Radical Loving Care* as his teaching guide. Accordingly, he has helped employee morale and patient satisfaction rise wherever he has led.

The core of Jason's success lies in his presence. He is a classic example of the opposite of an "energy thief." When he comes into a meeting the light rises and everyone in the room feels better.

Jason Barker refuses to motivate using fear. Instead, he lives love. That is why he will always be a success.

PRESENCE IN HOSPITALS

Ten Seconds

How can the power of presence energize a team?

It was the second "Code Blue" of the night for a medical resident at Massachusetts General Hospital. The case occurred years ago but she remembers it clearly. When she arrived at the scene the paddles had been applied to the patient's chest twice. She pitched in to help as best she could.

Shoulder-to-shoulder with her team, she labored desperately for five more minutes. But, the patient, a sixty-year old grandmother, was unresponsive. The physician in charge called off further efforts. The patient was dead.

The group dispersed. But, the resident lingered. Why was the wonderful team who had moments before been fighting together to save a life now walking off as if none of it mattered? In an editorial in the *New England Journal of Medicine* she asked healthcare leaders across America a question: When a patient dies after a Code Blue could the team linger for just *ten more seconds* to honor the life of the person who has just died?

The then-young medical resident was asking for presence by team members to the lifeless body before them and by team members to each other. She was asking that leaders adjust Code protocols, just slightly, to humanize a hard experience. To my knowledge, no leaders have listened to her.

> *Pay attention, don't let life go by you. Fall in love with the back of a cereal box.*
>
> Jerry Seinfeld

What forces militate against genuine presence? The modern day equivalent of television is, of course, the challenge to presence offered by the computer and smart phone. I know one teenager who had so much trouble gaining her father's attention that she finally called his cell phone, and he was sitting on the other side of the dinner table.

Practice what my dad called "The Gospel of Interruption." Anxious as you are to dash off to work, pause for a sincere goodbye to your family.

Rushed as you may feel on your way to a meeting, stop and listen when someone approaches you.

Your attention demonstrates who and what you value. When someone tells you repeatedly that they are too busy to talk with you or answer your emails that signals their communication with you is not important. When you show up to someone and make true eye contact you are engaging one of your greatest powers, the gift of your full presence.

THE MOST TRANSFORMATIVE PRACTICE FOR PRESENCE

One practice that will transform your ability to be present to yourself as well as to others is simple and powerful. Yet, few engage this easy pathway to peace with the exception of one important group of caregivers.

Did you ever wonder why so many nuns and sisters project such grace and presence? One big reason is that they take significant time each day to practice prayer and meditation.

As I wrote earlier, even if you meditate for as little as one minute a day it will help you. But if you practice simple meditation for twenty minutes twice a day you will be amazed at how full and beautiful your life will become.

Sit up straight in a chair. Pick a simple sound to repeat to yourself. Close your eyes. That is basically it.

A couple other guidelines help. When you hear other sounds, car horns or phones, let them go by. Breathe and focus on your breathing. When you are done, open your eyes slowly and rise gradually. Most important, when lists and worries disturb your peace ("monkey mind") let the sound you have chosen repeat itself. Engage the sound and gain relief from your monkey mind.

Initially, you will not feel like this is worth your time. Try it for a couple days, perhaps over the weekend. See how you feel.

After that, start your meetings with five minutes of quiet. Be sure people know to use a repeated sound to free the monkey mind. If you keep this going it is guaranteed to improve concentration, peace of mind and presence for you and your staff.

WHAT ARE YOU WAITING FOR?

What will you do in those hours between waking and sleeping? Will you be fully present for life or will you mortgage your life to distraction?

If you are looking for a current day example of being present to your life look again at the radical loving leadership of Toby Cosgrove. His life is packed with the kind of accomplishment that makes one wonder if he has ever slept.

> *We live between the act of awakening and the act of surrender. Each morning we awaken to the light and the invitation to a new day in the world of time; each night we surrender to the dark to be taken to play in the world of dreams where time is no more.*
>
> John O'Donohue

What alarms will awaken *you* to the life you were meant to live instead of the life you may be living now, frantic responses to the demands in front of you, battles through traffic, shallow dips into life's beauty, never, perhaps, experiencing what your life could be if you made a commitment to loving leadership.

Your partners, like you, are equipped with finely tuned weather gear. They watch which way the wind is blowing and can often sense the tiniest changes in barometric pressure.

Dr. Cosgrove's vast team draw energy when they see how committed he is. He has taken them on a bold new voyage instead of simply sailing to the old places.

Heed that inner voice that has been calling to you like the snooze alarm. You turn it off, it rings again, you turn it off again. How many times will you hit the snooze button before you finally rise to meet the best part of yourself, perhaps for the first time? Or will you stay asleep until your life ends?

Absent a stirring vision like the one Toby Cosgrove has championed at The Cleveland Clinic there is a high risk you will do what so many others have done, plod along from one day to the next until one day you fall into a semi-conscious retirement. What, then, will you be able say you have accomplished?

Each team member needs to take The Mother Test into their hearts, to make it their personal journey, not just yours. Most people use ten to twenty percent of their energy. A personal commitment will lift that number to ninety or one hundred percent. That is exactly how organizations reach the 99th percentile in patient and associate satisfaction!

Good employees placed on average teams may lower their game. Average employees who join a peak performing team quickly try to raise their game to match their peers. Hospital culture is peer behavior. You and your peers determine the culture in which you live.

Exceptional performers employed by mediocre teams find it hard to continue outperforming, and thus "showing up" their peers. They can do it, but as in the story I told earlier about the hospital receptionist who "made her co-workers look bad," their peers will try hard to pull them down.

When the good employees dominate, the poor ones fade. The dominant group tips the team toward excellence. This is how leaders change culture, one employee and one team at a time. During bold voyages many want to mutiny. If you do not face resistance your vision is not bold enough.

Lincoln and Mother Teresa were introverts. Roosevelt and King were more extroverted.

It is not extroversion that matters it is a positive *presence* and sincerity. Public speaking and rounding require your best presence, even when you are talking to a small group or sailing through the hallways.

Many leaders of giant companies (Howard Shultz at Starbucks, for example) make it a point to show up regularly with front line staff. They are NOT doing this as "undercover bosses." They are open and forthright about it.

BEST ROUNDING QUESTIONS

Ask first line staff or other leaders: How do you give loving care?

This is the single best inquiry I have ever made. Some people start by responding, "I don't know. I just do it." But if you stay with the questions they will give you some beautiful answers.

The multiple values of this question include: 1) showing that you respect the individual by being interested in their views, 2) signaling what *you* value (loving care, not just policies, budgets and chart completion, 3) giving the other person a chance to teach *you* what loving care means to them.

Ask about family. You do not need to be pals with every member of your staff. You *do* need to show you care. That is what you want in your hospital, caring.

If you are not great at names get the appropriate executive to change name tags so that the first name appears large. We did this at both Riverside Methodist and Baptist.

Thank staff for their hard work and for being there even if you know nothing about their work record. No one ever told me, "You should not have thanked that nurse. She's a bad employee."

Good rounding *raises energy* and directly affects culture in positive ways. Bad rounding or no rounding does the reverse. If you are spending all your time in meetings or in your office you are as bad a leader as a President of the United States who would never leave The White House.

SUPERSTARS AT ROUNDING

The healthcare leaders profiled here are outstanding at rounding. Toby Cosgrove first learned his rounding skills as a physician visiting patients. He has transferred that experience brilliantly to his leadership encounters with first line staff.

> *Culture counts. No strategic plan can work if an organization's culture is not aligned with the initiative.*
>
> Richard Cordoba –
> CEO Children's
> Hospital Los Angeles

Laurie Harting (formerly Laurie Eberst) knows how to bring forward her best self in rounding and in the rest of her leadership. A former CNO, she knows how it feels on the front lines.

She was so successful building a culture of loving care at Mercy Gilbert in Arizona (following the book Radical Loving Care to a tee) that she was promoted to run the three-hospital group, part of Dignity Health, based at St. John's Hospital in Oxnard, California. Once again, she did that job so well she was promoted to her current position in Sacramento.

You can sense the positive energy Laurie generates as soon as she comes onto a patient floor. She listens to her staff, knows them by name, and offers powerful affirmations. When she introduced me during one visit I remember watching her step back and smile at her team with all the pride of a great coach.

During his tenure as CEO at St. Ann's Hospital in Apple Valley, California and later at St. Vincent Hospital in Billings, Montana Jason Barker's balance of compassion and competence resulted in each organization rocketing to record levels of performance in most areas. He has regularly used Radical Loving Care as a teaching guide for himself and the many leaders and caregivers he has managed.

Jason is a champion. He has always brought his best presence to rounding because he knows that is part of his job. As a result, the people who have worked for him consistently passed The Mother Test and the patients they have served were the beneficiaries of his peak performing leadership.

Jason, Laurie, Jim, Joel, Nancy, George, every one of our leaders is a superstar at rounding. And every one of the hospitals they lead has felt the benefits of their leadership.

WORKING ALONGSIDE YOUR TEAMS

I used to don the uniform of a first line staff member every month. If you do this, you had better be sincere. Condescension of any kind is a killer.

This approach worked incredibly well, most of the time.

About twelve years into this practice, I made a mistake of arrogance. I was working in the dish room at Baptist with an eleven-year veteran named Darren. Washing away, I started thinking what a humble fellow I was for leaving my cushy office, taking off my coat and tie and dipping my hands into the very hot water. I began feeling prouder and prouder of myself until I asked a question.

"What do you like best about this job, Darren?"

"What I like best is working alone," he told me as he watched me repeatedly put dishes and pans in the wrong place.

I laughed and got out of Darren's way. The first line staff does the hardest work in the hospital. Work with them and also try to stay out of their way.

No patient cares what is happening in the C-suite. No one being admitted asks, "Have you got enough executives here?"

John O'Donohue offers this two-line prayer: "As a river flows in ideal sequence / May your soul discover time is presence."

Caregivers matter most to patients. Leadership presence matters most to caregivers.

The Seventh Power
APPLYING PEACE, GRATITUDE and HUMILITY

Gratitude is the mother of joy.
Forgiveness is the father of grace.
Humility is the child of love.
These three are the family of peace.

PROFILE IN PEACE AND HUMILITY

Many years ago Dr. George Mikitarian, the top notch President and CEO of Parrish Medical, was among the first leaders in the country to fully engage the Radical Loving Care approach. In doing so, he extended an invitation to his staff to embrace major culture change.

> To survive in life you need three bones. A wishbone, a backbone and a funny bone.
>
> Reba McIntire

Over the next several years George and his team transformed culture and Parrish became stronger in almost every area. But some medical staff issues remained.

As he addressed those issues, George proved over and over that he has a backbone as well as a wishbone and a funny bone. To deal with medical staff quality, George made a courageous decision.

In a key battle, he engineered the removal of a disruptive physician who was a significant admitter to the hospital and popular among some of his peers. As many had warned, the census dropped, the hospital lost money and the doctor sued the hospital.

But, George remained a model of inner peace amid an organizational storm. He successfully sent a powerful message: Parrish will not tolerate substandard performance or abusive doctors. Excellence is required, not simply requested.

Over the next several months George led his staff through a dangerous forest and into a new land of success. Some new physicians joined the staff, bad ones left, nursing confidence in the sincerity of top leadership soared, patient satisfaction rose and the hospital returned to profitability.

A few years later another crisis struck. The NASA installation that supplied most of the jobs in the area closed. The impact on nearby Parrish was significant.

Once again, George remained calm. He made more tough, high-purpose decisions. Since then, he has once again led the organization back to success and Parrish is now ranked among the top ten hospitals in Florida.

Some organizations use different language for this work. Yet, in every case, the key change agents have been capable leaders like George generating successful performance against a Mother Test type of standard.

The first winner of the Healing Hospital award went to Parrish Medical Center because of George—who was subsequently selected as Healing Hospital CEO of the Year. Yet, he remains a profoundly humble human being. He wants excellence around him so he promotes and hires to accomplish that. The community, as well as patients and visitors, consistently receive the best because George brings the best out of his staff.

Dr. George Mikitarian demonstrates that inner peace fuels successful leadership on the healthcare stage just as it does on the world stage.

In answer to a question about her mission to "the poorest of the poor" Mother Teresa said "I followed Jesus into the slums." She yielded to a higher voice.

Inner peace is the hardest of the seven powers to learn. Most leaders who lead from inner peace have stepped back and looked at larger forces beyond themselves. They align themselves with a higher power. This brings humility because humility needs inner acceptance.

> *If you are humble nothing will touch you, neither praise nor disgrace, because you know what you are.*
>
> Mother Teresa

The most peace-centered leader I ever worked with is Tracy Wimberly. She even had a small sign that read "Peace" on the door to her office. Her presence could calm the most upset doctor or staff member. As a result, people were drawn to her leadership presence.

Doctors are terrific at projecting a calm demeanor. No one, obviously, wants her or his surgeon to appear in the waiting room screaming: "Oh my god, the blood in there was everywhere!"

Doctors ground their confidence in three ways—their technical training, their experience, and the medical school teaching about professional demeanor. This approach builds patient confidence but it does not always bring peace to the doctor.

When a surgeon throws a tantrum, and instruments, it means fear or fatigue has pushed peace to the sidelines.

Leaders can use the same tools of technical training, experience, and teaching. Inner peace lies deeper. It requires constant mining to tap the well of peace's precious waters.

You can see inner peace emerging in the face of Martin Luther King when you watch him deliver the last several paragraphs of his "I Have A Dream" speech. You can see the same sense of inner certainty when you see film of Roosevelt intoning, amid the Depression, "The only thing we have to fear is fear itself."

Inner peace is what enables real presence.

Deep purpose fuels calm and certainty.

INNER PEACE DURING CRISES?

If you can keep your head when all about you
are losing theirs and blaming it on you. . .

Rudyard Kipling

A strange thing about peace in each of us is that it can be situational. Sometimes peace rises within us and feels permanent. Other times, it eludes us. An odd phenomenon in my psyche is that I am sometimes calmer in crisis than I am when someone is talking loudly on a plane.

MURDER

December 30, 1983, would be the last day on earth for Patricia Matix, a talented and dedicated young researcher at Riverside Methodist Hospital. She was a mother of a two month old. Her husband was a Vietnam Veteran. He would die within three years.

Joyce McFadden, Pat's equally capable colleague, could not know that five days earlier, she had celebrated her last Christmas.

In the village that is a hospital every person is either sick or supporting someone who is. Staff members are accustomed to almost every kind of emergency. But no one expects a murder in a place where people come to be saved.

By 4:45 p.m. the winter sky had darkened. In the middle of the holidays some leaders had left work early.

Dr. Ed Bope, head of our Family Practice Residency, walked into my office ashen-faced. "Erie, one of our employees has been murdered down the hall in the research lab," he said.

"Are you sure she's dead? " I heard myself ask. "Did you call a code?"

"When you see her, you will know why I didn't check. She has bled out."

Our chief operating officer, a Colonel in the Army Reserve, clasped his hands to his head and said, "Oh my God, what are we going to do?"

"The first thing is I want you to do is to go into your office, close the door, and calm down," I told him.

Before starting down the hall to the murder scene my secretary called security and our Vice President, Frank Pandora, to meet me at the research lab fifty steps away.

In my years as a defense lawyer, prosecutor, judge as well as watching surgeries and helping out in the ER, I had never seen anything like the sight on the other side of the laboratory door. On the floor, gagged, her hands and feet tied behind her back, was the body of poor, sweet Joyce McFadden. Pooled around her was every drop of her blood, the tissue that moments before had vitalized her body.

Leaders don't have the luxury of mourning for more than a moment when the safety of more than two thousand patients and caregivers is suddenly at risk. Part of the mind wants to adopt the detective role—to try to solve the murder mystery.

But this true story challenges you in a different way. What would you do if you were a hospital leader in this situation, not Sherlock Holmes?

In minutes we assembled the crew needed to run the hospital amid a crisis. This included leaders who would travel the floors to offer reassurance and encouragement and, before the days of cell phones, runners to carry messages.

The police were notified. The moment that happened, the message of murder blared through police radios to the news media and thus to the public. What if the family were listening?

Rather than use the PA system, we drafted a written communication offering reassurance and basic facts to staff. Before we sent it out, something else occurred.

How Could Things Turn Worse?

Minutes after the police arrived, Frank Pandora, the Vice President I had left in charge at the scene, called.

"Are you sitting down, Erie?" he asked me. "I have terrible news."

How could any news be more tragic than a murder? The answer fell fast.

"The police just found another body," Frank said. "Her name is Patricia Matix. Her body was in the lab freezer, killed the same way."

Our census sheet showed that six hundred seventy-nine patients lay in hospital beds. Thirty more were receiving care in our emergency department.

We had set up three centers, a command center based in my office area, another office area with enough rooms to handle family members in separate groups and a third space to deal with the media. As a dozen people assembled in the executive area I noticed how quiet everyone was, all looking my way to see what to do next. Oddly, I felt a sense of inner peace much more than on an ordinary day. "We're going to get through this just fine," I said.

But, cool, decisive *action* brings calm best. The circumstance was not unlike a war setting. Two of our "soldiers" had been killed. The enemy may be in the halls looking for more victims.

The message I spoke to a waiting crowd of reporters had three basic elements:

"We are saddened to report that two of our beloved staff members have been murdered in the research area of the hospital." (Compassion)

"We are confident the crimes were *confined to this limited area* and patient care is not affected. All patients and staff are safe and are being cared for normally." (Reassurance)

"Since this is a police matter, here is Captain Johnson who will address all of those issues." (Separation of the criminal matter from hospital operations.)

Through this communication, we expressed the tender-hearted tough-minded approach. The hospital ran smoothly and public confidence in the hospital was unaffected. Patients, staff and doctors continued to trust us. Once the police took over we compartmentalized the problem. A tragedy was managed successfully.

[The subsequent events are collateral to hospital leadership. However, three years later the murderer and his partner Bill Matix (the husband of our murdered employee Patricia Matix) went on a killing spree through Florida. In a shoot-out in Orlando, FBI agents killed them. Two agents also died and others were wounded. The entire story was the subject of an NBC drama, "The FBI Murders."]

HOSTAGES

> *When adversity strikes, that's when you have to be the most calm. Take a step back, stay strong, stay grounded and press on.*
>
> LL Cool J

Amazingly, just six months later a different crisis struck Riverside Methodist. A prisoner/patient in the outpatient section of the hospital grabbed a gun from a guard and took the guard hostage.

The leadership challenge once again became a matter of isolating the incident from patient care and organizing a professional response. As news and police helicopters circled the hospital, communication and calm once again became paramount. One phrase I *never* use is to tell people, "Don't panic." Negative phrasing produces the wrong result. Tell people not to panic and they will. Reassure them that the situation is under control.

We sealed off the area and issued regular announcements that the crisis was limited to one room where the criminal was isolated (Based on the prior crisis our credibility was strong.) We emphasized that patient care would continue normally.

There was more chaos this time than with the murders. The city police were there. The governor called me offering the highway patrol. Simultaneously a large group of prison guards gathered to offer support to their captured colleague.

Finally, the mayor appeared personally. Public officials are not always helpful. The mayor suggested, "Why don't we think about smoking this guy out?"

After I pointed out that the smoke would quickly travel from the basement through the vents and scare everyone in the hospital he said, "Oh, I hadn't thought of that."

The story took another light-hearted turn when the police negotiator used a trick I did not think would work. She convinced the prisoner to trade bullets for pills.

After a steady dose of tranquilizers and painkillers, a strange and welcome sound arose, snoring. The prisoner had fallen asleep! He was quickly arrested and the crisis was defused.

As in the case of the murders, the goal was to continue to signal to the public that Riverside Methodist was a safe place to come. The best proof was the fact that the crisis was over. The media accepted this, with one significant exception.

Our public relations officer, Maryln Marr, advised that a reporter for *The Columbus Dispatch* planned to run a story suggesting Riverside was "cursed."

Never try to talk a reporter out of running a story. They will simply report that you are trying to block the truth. Instead, we invited a well-respected doctor to contact the publisher with the message that such a report would scare patients unnecessarily. The publisher killed the story.

When practicing for crises, imagine yourself into the likely panic in the situation. Practice your ability to remain centered and effective.

A WALK OUT

While attending a conference in Chicago I received a call from Columbus that our Radiology Department had threatened a walk-out. Treatment at Riverside Methodist, the largest hospital in Ohio, might grind to a standstill.

By the time VPs Mark Evans and Marian Hamm greeted me at the airport most of the Radiology staff had refused to report for work. Only a skeleton staff remained to sustain the most critical operations.

The overall issue was wages not working condition. It was a Friday. Our attorney correctly warned against meeting with wildcat strikers. Nevertheless, I believe in face-to-face communication and scheduled a Sunday meeting with them.

Since it was a weekend it seemed likely some would bring their children. As the meeting began it was clear many had done exactly that. I had done the same. My then-teenage daughter was with me.

The room was packed. I knew some of the technologists because I had worked alongside them in my rounding. A few glared. Others looked sheepish.

How do you defuse tension and gain common ground with angry opponents?

Scout Finch taught me an answer. Remember the scene in *To Kill A Mockingbird* when Atticus is confronted at the jail by a mob that wants to lynch his client? That scene was defused when his daughter, Scout, appeared and spoke directly to one of the adults she knew. Instantly, the tension eased and the crowd broke up. Childhood innocence converted the face of the mob from angry to kind.

That is the main reason my daughter was with me. My other reason was to show her a challenging part of leadership.

The first things I did were to thank the group and to introduce my daughter. The next was to tell them I appreciated their hard work and knew they were committed to the patients that needed their help.

Carla, one of those who had glared, said, "Look, we are not being paid enough. What are you going to do about it?"

"Carla, I wish we could pay you and everyone here a million dollars a year," I answered. Faces softened. A few chuckled. "Caregiving is what matters and I respect how hard you work. I promise to look at this but I cannot promise we will change your pay. No hospital can ever pay what caregiving is worth. But, you deserve the best we can do."

After a few more minutes I closed the meeting by saying. "Thank you all for meeting with me on a Sunday. You all care about your families. The sick people here are desperate for your help. I know you won't let them down. See you tomorrow."

I'm not sure if it was the appeal to patient care or my daughter humanizing the face of "the enemy" or the promise to consider their request but the next day, most returned. A "mob" is made up of individuals. We met with them individually and thanked them again for their work.

Instead of pay increases we produced proof that their pay was at or above comparable technologists in the area. Most were unaware of that. By the end of the week, the department was fully staffed again. Trouble never returned.

HOW DIFFERENT LEADERS REACT TO CRISIS

As a student of leadership psychology it is fascinating to watch leaders in crisis. In the murder crisis three top Vice Presidents reacted differently. The Chief Financial Officer left mid-crisis later saying (oddly) that he did not think the crisis had much to do with finance. The Chief Operating Officer briefly decompensated. The Chief Legal Officer, Frank Pandora, responded like a champion.

Watch leaders in crisis. According to first-hand reports, the CEO at one Tennessee hospital set new heights for fear-based leadership amid trouble. During two separate bomb threats he had a security officer drive him as far from the hospital as possible. He then called the executive in charge for an update. He told one of his staff, "I don't think the CEO should be placed at risk if a bomb went off, do you?"

If you want a model of how to lead in crises as well as everyday look again at George Mikitarian. When inner threats and outer attacks have arisen he has projected a strength and calm that can only arise from inner peace.

INNER PEACE WITH YOUR LEADER

My therapist told me the way to achieve true inner peace is to finish what I start. So far today I have finished two bags of M and Ms and a chocolate cake. I feel better already.

Dave Barry

So many bosses scare the daylights out of their staff. They create daily emergencies in the hearts of team members who chronically fear being fired.

270

The Dave Barry approach probably looks more appealing than a sermon about inner peace. You cannot control your boss's mood but you can manage yours. You cannot control the behavior of your partners or which patients will be rushed through the ER door but you can influence this significantly.

If you spend your hours only reacting to outward events with surface energy you will never develop your deeper strengths. What if you engage the courage of a pioneer to dig wells into the waters of your soul? What if you use the wisdom of a settler to nurture the springs that rise up?

But, is that really going to work? If you cannot stand your boss, look hard for another job. Meanwhile, focus your attention on the energy source within rather than getting yanked around from without. How have you labeled yourself and your boss? Find new labels and you may find more peace.

The stories you tell about yourself shape your energy. They cannot teach you if you do not figure out what they are. Create a new and better story for yourself. Help others do the same. Spot those who never thought they were leaders, affirm them and then appoint them to positions where they thrive.

One of your best tools is affirmation. Mother Teresa summarizes this point well. "Kind words can be short and easy to speak, but their echoes are truly endless."

Affirm the strengths of your team members and they will become stronger. Focus on their problems and they will become weaker and more afraid of making mistakes.

John O'Donohue is always eloquent: "As clay anchors a tree in light and wind/May your outer life grow from peace within."

If you are wise enough to visit Parrish Medical Center you may well feel a sense of inner peace as soon as you enter the main lobby. Light streams through large windows. Light comes through the eyes of front desk staff and nurses on the floors.

Dr. George Mikitarian and his team designed Parrish Medical Center to be a place that would offer inner peace to frightened patients and their families. He has designed his staff the same way by picking leaders who practice compassion as well as competence.

George has always wanted Parrish to be more than a hospital. He has strived to make sure it is a model of healing, a place where the sick and wounded can find peace as well as a cure.

Find inner peace and you will help others find their own.

Why Some Hospitals Fail The Mother Test

Mission Excellence or Mission Fraud?

BOARD RESPONSIBILITY

Boards are at the top of the organization chart. On rare occasions, they need to be at the top of the action chart as well. Their most important job is to ensure mission advancement by picking the right CEO. After that they are stewards of overall vision. The time for action comes when it is clear that mission performance is breaking down and vision has gone flat.

Over the past forty years I have been fortunate to work alongside outstanding board members, particularly at Riverside Methodist Hospital and at OhioHealth.

An outstanding board supports superior performance. The boards I have served as CEO supported breakthrough efforts that led to exceptional results. The same has been true at all organizations that deliver high purpose excellence. When boards establish high standards, patient care improves, employees thrive, the best physicians deliver care, the finest leaders lead and financial performance is often exceptional.

Excellent boards insist on excellence.

Every board approves grand mission statements to provide the best care for all. They need to be sure that mission is being lived out. Boards at the top hospitals profiled here do that well. Some other hospital boards allow subpar performance. Are they involved in mission fraud?

MR. SUBPAR

"James" was CEO of the same hospital for ten years. During that time he was routinely outperformed by his competitors, gradually lost his best physicians to other hospitals, saw his patient satisfaction drop into the twenties and his employee turnover rate rise to nearly thirty percent.

After repeatedly being unable or unwilling to follow good counsel he was finally let go. He had lasted a decade *because the hospital's board of directors tolerated his mediocrity year after year.*

THE PITFALLS OF ARROGANCE, GREED AND IRRITABILITY

Much of the media thrives on the scandalous and arrogant behavior of leaders and stars. Hospitals are flooded with stories of arrogant and greedy leaders, doctors having affairs and caregivers covering up deadly mistakes.

In the context of this book, we care about private behavior when it gets in the way of leaders being their best selves and causing Mother Test failures. Still, even when the behavior does not cause failures you, as a leader, need to learn the pitfalls.

Everyone knows the line from Lord Acton about how power corrupts and absolute power corrupts absolutely. But, numerous leaders often turn a blind eye to this wisdom when power starts changing their behavior. The problem gets worse if the leader is tyrannical because subordinates become fearful of pointing out the problem.

$25,000

In the 1980s Dan, the head of a large Ohio hospital, could not keep his hands out of the hospital coffers. For example, personal home improvements were charged to the hospital. The CFO was believed to be complicit in this misuse of funds.

In one specific example Dan admitted to me that he took a $25,000 bonus and ran it through the hospital books as an expense to avoid paying taxes. Employee morale was terrible. Patient satisfaction was low. Some teams were still passing The Mother Test but many were failing.

Dan, of course, was paying no attention to any of that.

Finally, the hospital crashed financially and was taken over. The CEO's illegal behavior did not stop. He committed fraud with a subsequent company and, as of this writing, is still in prison.

Importantly, as soon as the hospital was taken over by competent leadership it began to thrive and is, today, an excellent center of care with a strong bottom line.

ROOFS AND RACISM

I saw behavior like Dan's at another large hospital in the South. Richard, the CEO, got the hospital to pay to replace the roof on his house and for other personal expenses. At another hospital the CEO was engaged in affairs with three employees at the same time. He also frequently ordered that employees be fired because he thought they were overweight or were men wearing earrings and gay.

This CEO became so notorious for his bizarre behavior that two exposes appeared in a local newspaper. In behavior suggestive of Richard Nixon and Watergate, the CEO allegedly had the investigative reporter followed. His "agent" reports included a racist description of the reporter as having a large "Jewish" nose!

Finally, a board committee was appointed to investigate. The CEO intimidated executives who were called as witnesses and the committee issued what one board member later called "a whitewashed report" exonerating the CEO.

The hospital's financials dived further into red ink. It was only saved from bankruptcy when new leadership took over.

"YOU'LL NEVER TAKE ME ALIVE"

Some stories of CEO behavior are hard to believe. They show how long many boards can take to correct situations that are clearly damaging.

One CEO running a California hospital began to show obvious signs of paranoia. The board was warned and ignored it. Finally, the board chair decided to confront the CEO

When he did, the CEO turned over his desk and blockaded himself in his office shouting, "You'll never take me alive."

SAFEGUARDS, SELF-GUARDS: A MIRROR TEST

Mirrors reflect a clear image of a particular kind. But, you may misread what you see.

There is no such thing as a flawless leader and no such thing as an employee reporting to you who is blind to your flaws. Yet, many leaders surround themselves with people who only tell them what they want to hear.

If your staff member cannot tell you a weakness that means he or she is scared of your reaction. Your best self requires that you know your faults before you can become a peak performer.

This approach starts with your humility and continues with a question in which you show concern for the boss and offer help. People have done this with me it helps me re-balance, when I listen. Unfortunately, sometimes, I have not.

The point is that you, like everyone, can go blind to your flaws. Leaders do not have this luxury. You need reasonable feedback approaches in order to work your way back into your best self.

I encouraged a specific member of my staff, Jeff Kaplan, to push back at me whenever he felt I was slipping into arrogance. A former assistant football coach under Woody Hayes, he knew how to be tough. He is also one of the best leaders I ever worked with.

SORTING OUT HARMLESS FROM HARMFUL

Leadership stories can also entertain.

Bruce Trumm was the beloved head of Toledo's Riverside Hospital in the early 1970s. He is the man who hired me out of the federal prosecutor's office and into healthcare.

Like Roosevelt, Bruce had suffered polio in his early twenties. The bad leg he developed caused him to slide his foot along the hallway so that it was hard to hear him coming. Thus, we gave him a nickname that he loved: "The Pink Panther."

A former executive at Owens Illinois Bruce was part of an age where three martini lunches were not uncommon. When I came to Riverside as a senior executive Bruce stationed me outside the boardroom each month during meetings. The sessions were held at lunchtime in a room next to the cafeteria.

At the first meeting I heard a cart clinking through that cafeteria. On it was a complete array of hard liquor. The employees were used to this sight. I was not.

Caregivers eating meatloaf and drinking ice tea in the middle of the day while board members downed martinis always laughed at "the booze cart." But they must have wondered about any business being transacted behind that closed door.

After a few months, Bruce asked me if I had any suggestions. "Well," I said timidly, "I'm not sure the booze cart is a good idea. After all, it is wheeled right through the cafeteria in front of all the employees."

"You don't like my booze cart, eh?" he boomed. "We'll see about that."

The next month I was at my post at the boardroom door. I had my back to the cafeteria when I heard an unusually loud round of laughter from the staff. I turned around. There was the booze cart, completely covered with a white sheet! When I turned back, there was The Pink Panther. I will never forget the grin on his face, "Well, Erie, what do you think about my solution?"

Funny as that was, after I became CEO the drink cart vanished, never to be seen again.

Although the positive results at the organizations I led reflect very successful leadership I made many mistakes. I do not offer myself as an ideal leader.

The healthcare television show I created was successful and became internationally syndicated. It benefited Riverside Methodist, OhioHealth and communities locally and around the country. But, did I have to name it "Life Choices with *Erie Chapman*?" I let my ego get the best of me.

Sometimes leadership behavior may be reprehensible but it may also be harmless to mission performance. The problem, however, can taint integrity.

There is no evidence that love affairs of Franklin D. Roosevelt and John F. Kennedy had any effect on the voyage of the Ship of State. Steven Jobs' notorious irritability with staff was outrageous. But, it was outweighed by his astonishing genius. Still, integrity matters and low integrity kills a leader's trust level in ways that can destroy the confidence of many followers.

Stories of leadership misbehavior need to be sorted into whether they affect organizational performance or not. If every doctor who had an affair were dismissed many medical staffs would lose some of their best members. It is patient care, clinical quality and responsible financial performance that matter.

WHO CAN ACT?

When there is leadership malfeasance or just plain negligence, there's not much a first line employee can do. There is a lot that other senior leaders can do but they usually do not. In one hospital a senior executive flew secretly to the home office of the hospital system and reported his CEO's misfeasance. The boss was subsequently fired.

But these acts of courage are rare. *The main responsibility rests with the board* and they are too often asleep or blinded by CEOs too clever to be caught.

Patients and employees deserve consistent excellence. The public is entitled to full value from their non-profit health care organizations. Bad care emerges when Boards tolerate leadership negligence.

WHAT BOARDS FAIL TO ACT?

Many CEOs have been in the job for decades. Across that time, the hospitals they lead have never accomplished anything different from any other ordinary hospitals. Yet, in every case, the hospitals could have done better by engaging good leadership.

There are any number of possible explanations for Board member negligence: 1) Board members are volunteers and do not want controversy. 2) Many subpar CEOs are brilliant at explaining their mistakes or blaming others, 3) Many hospital board members do not understand their role, 4) If board members are status quo

> *It is not uncommon for people to spend their whole life waiting to start living.*
>
> Eckhart Tolle

leaders themselves they may be comfortable with average performance, 5) The members like the status of serving on the board and are fearful they will be pushed off if they express concern, 6) Board members think the hospital should improve but they are too fearful or unmotivated to act, or 7) They may have a direct conflict of interest.

Board members do act in many situations. But, too often, they sit back and do nothing. Some of them have never been fully present in their own work. In Tolle's words, they have spent "their whole life waiting to start living."

WHAT CAN THE BOARD DO?

Boards of Directors act through the CEO. One of the most important things they do is to hire or fire him or her. After that, it is their job to oversee performance. It is *not* their job to micromanage and board members who do that cause as much trouble as board members who do nothing.

A good chair is the best way to ensure good CEO performance. This means a chair that pays attention, supports and affirms a great job, offers constructive suggestions to solve problems and does *not* micromanage.

Across my career I have sat through hundreds of board meetings—in public, for profit corporations as well as in non-profit hospitals. It is astounding to me how few board members ask meaningful questions.

As with every other area, where attention goes, energy flows. Board inattention puts hospitals at risk. Honestly, I liked it when board members were more passive because that left me with one less thing to worry about. But, active interest contributes to healthy organizations.

Boards of directors are stewards of organizational mission. Board support can do wonders for the energy and performance of a CEO and the organization. In addition, every good board should welcome an occasional outside presentation and performance review of the board as a whole. Every bad board should fear one.

A Final Word to CEOs

What lies behind us and what lies ahead of us are tiny matters compared to what lives within us.

Henry David Thoreau

A NEW RADICAL LOVING LEADER

In the still-new millennium a bright image of Radical Loving Leadership has emerged among us. Like all loving leaders, Pope Francis has his flaws. His towering example of hope and change rises above any human failings. He set the tone for all leaders at the beginning of his papacy. "Let us never forget that authentic power is service..." This is a clarion call to you and to all of us. In spite of margin pressures your top responsibility is *mission* not margins.

Part of the reason I have offered so much advice to you is that I have made countless mistakes in my career and in my life along with scoring successes. For example, I can see that toward the end of my twelve years heading OhioHealth some level of complacency and arrogance slipped into my leadership behavior. With so many constantly telling me how great I was I made the mistake of believing too much and lost balance. Complacency and arrogance are twin risks for CEOs.

In Roman times, conquering generals peacocked through the streets of Rome to celebrate their triumphs. To counter their cockiness Caesar required that a slave stand next to the general in his chariot. The slave's role was to whisper into the general's ear "All glory is fleeting." Some authorities claim this tradition lasted for centuries. Jeff Kaplan and others on my staff tried to perform a similar role by warning me every so often. Towards the end, I started to ignore them. Make sure a member of your staff is there to keep you balanced. Listen to that person!

Since I have been in your kind of job, I know how it feels to carry the weight of the organization on your shoulders and how hard it is to stay in your best self all the time.

Competence may seem far more important than compassion. It is not, especially when you are running a caregiving organization. Competence and compassion are of equal value.

Even though coaches and politicians and military leaders use it, it may be difficult for you to utter the "love" word. But, what power is greater than love? Listen to how other leaders use it and it may free you to engage love language in your leadership. Remember that you lead caregivers not Marines heading into battle. If loving leadership is good for soldiers it is even more important for nurses and doctors and other therapists.

Want to hear the best advice I have? It comes from an old veteran:

❖ Love your staff.
❖ Love patients.
❖ Love doctors.
❖ Love your work.

> *My continuing passion is to part a curtain,*
> *that invisible veil of indifference*
> *that falls between us*
> *and that blinds us to each other's presence,*
> *each other's wonder,*
> *each other's human plight.*
>
> Eudora Welty

Love from your mother and father may have been the most important leadership training you ever received. Sometimes, to get in touch with your best self means reuniting with your childhood self. Back then, you hoped for compassion when you were hurt.

Your best self is your loving self. That is what your leadership seeks in others.

No team can pass The Mother Test with superficial gestures recited by rote. Your healing efforts must flow from a personal place of caring. Can you work with a team member whom you do not like? Can you perform for a boss you fear?

These situations can become a new story. The cranky doctor could be a fellow being who is afraid. Your "dislikable" leader may have suffered from a bad upbringing. Your boss may never have learned another way to lead except with fear.

Redefine your "why" so that it stirs you out of your current patterns into new ones.

Typical motivators include the following:

Pride: I want to be the best. **Money:** I need it. **Power:** I want it. **Duty:** I have to do it. **Fear:** I do not want to get fired.

How can you wed the hopes and dreams of everyone to the higher purpose of better care for the sick and wounded?

THE WISDOM OF "I DON'T KNOW."

Buddhists revere the Dalai Lama as their leader. He is honored by millions of others for his wisdom and fine sense of humor. After giving a speech at the University of Colorado he fielded questions from the audience.

Parker Palmer reports that one man rose with an inquiry. Excited at the opportunity to address the great man he went on and on. As Palmer pointed out, "People who ask long, rambling 'questions' don't really stop. They sort of subside, as the surf does now and then."

Finally, the man got to a question. How can my wife and I raise our three small children?

After a pause, the Dalai Lama spoke: "How should I know? I MONK!"

How refreshing.

In some ways, I feel odd about offering you "all the answers." How should I know what you are dealing with?

Leaders often think they are supposed to have the answer to every question. So often, the best and most courageous response for us is also the honest one: "I don't know."

But, clearly, you are the one people look to for the big answers.

Your Headlines

If your life were being reported in a newspaper of your own writing what would the headlines be? The newspaper reports what has happened. Accidents and illnesses, for example, have already written themselves into your heart.

Your personal news reports what you have done in response to your setbacks and how you have dealt with your successes. These stories include what steps you have taken forward or backward. The late television star and best-selling author Art Linkletter (an old family friend) wrote, "Things turn out best for people who make the best of the way things turn out."

Can you reshape stories that have been weighing you down? How much of your life energy is being blocked by anger over someone who betrayed you?

How do you want the new news of your life to read?

FROM ORDINARY TO EXCELLENT –
THE NEW STANDARD

As you now know, the goal of The Mother Test is easy to state and hard enough so that only the best leaders can pass it. As you can see, the leaders profiled here show that you, too, can pass the test.

> *The top job of a healthcare leader is to take care of the people who take care of people.*

Leaders should do more than simply retain the capable people that are meeting this high standard. They should recognize, reward and support peak performing caregivers in every way that makes sense.

Successful hospitals prove that The Mother Test works regardless of the size or location of the organization.

Remember that only a clear and compelling vision can create meaningful change. Martin Luther King's vision was bold and straightforward: To end segregation in the south. Imagine if his vision had been, "We need to improve relations in the south." If your vision is "we want to give better care" you will not motivate a single person.

Healthcare organizations are transformed with a straightforward, sophisticated and persistent implementation of one standard: The Mother Test.

Your vision must help you move the bureaucracy.

Look inside healthcare organizations that are failing The Mother Test and you will see leaders who have forgotten that their purpose is to serve the sick. They may have ignored Jim Skogsbergh's warning to "keep your eyes on the prize."

The quickest way to develop a culture that passes The Mother Test: Raise the bar. Then redevelop, remove and reward.

Redevelop your team using this standard.

Remove or retrain the staff that is failing.

Reward those who you want caring for your loved ones.

HOW LONG DOES IT TAKE?

It takes at least one year to notice changes. Three years for real change. That is the guideline most people use for larger organizations.

At the midpoint in your journey some change will become visible. You are through the forest and the new land you have discovered is under cultivation.

If your initial action steps are still meeting resistance you will know you are on the right track. At the same time, listen carefully to skeptics who may have good recommendations.

In every organization where I have extended this invitation to radical excellence it took a year before meaningful change appeared. Because of the size of the organizations I led it often took three years before the culture of excellence was planted deeply.

Keep piloting new ideas and new skills. Come back later to the book and check steps you may have missed.

Success in each of the five relationships turns on your performance. Better patient care and better success in all departments will only come when vision becomes action and action starts bringing better results. Pilot your ideas before making broad ranging changes.

It may also be painful to admit that a given plan will never work. We spent many years at Riverside Methodist trying to redesign a new patient gown that could be worn with less embarrassment and more dignity. We never quite pulled that off.

One day it dawned on me that we had aimed our energy in the wrong direction. What was more important than a new patient gown was a new way of looking at the people wearing the gown.

In the hospital hierarchy, the "power" people are doctors wearing scrubs. Patients weakened by illness and lying on gurneys look for all the world like the *least* important people in the hospital.

Most hotels, restaurants and other retail operations have solved this problem. "Customers' are to be treated like kings or queens.

A happy patient once told me after discharge from Riverside Methodist, "You run a nice hotel." Really? Contrast the hospital model against the hotel model. Imagine being checked into a Holiday Inn and being told there will be a stranger in the room with you.

Most healthcare organizations have not yet solved this challenge.

SUCCESS AND FAILURE

> *Do or do not.*
> *There is no try.*
>
> Yoda

Southwest Airlines is a fine example of a culture of caring in a huge company that is cited all the time. This vast organization has achieved broad ranging success across every category because they have done basic things superbly. These include establishing a culture that mixes compassion with high competence, simplifying their systems as much as possible and focusing obsessively on hiring, orienting, training and reviewing *all* staff according to Mother Test-type standards.

Ordinary leaders always have excuses for why they their organization has not achieved big goals. Peak performing leaders focus on setting a vision, designing clear goals, and making it happen.

Weak leaders look for excuses not to act. When I cited the Southwest example to one hospital CEO he said to me: "Hospitals are much more complex. We are saving lives."

Flying planes carrying millions of passengers through the air is not only dangerous but also complicated.

Success and failure are not black and white concepts. Success with The Mother Test offers a complex and nuanced picture of performance. Some say you can only pass this test if you have a small organization. But, even *the largest of organizations can be broken down into teams* that in turn are made up of individuals.

Success comes when every team leader makes sure that every member is someone she trusts caring for a loved one. This is an achievable goal and you and your team can reach it.

THE MOTHER TEST CONTINUUM

"We are never going to be able to bring every leader on board," a Senior Vice President at a large hospital told me when I described what it took to pass The Mother Test. She looked defeated already.

Fortunately, you do not need "everybody" on board at the beginning or even in the middle of your journey to excellence. **Put The Mother Test**

on a continuum using the old school grading system. Evaluate your current teams and figure out roughly where you stand right now.

F——50% of staff failing

C——70% of staff passing

A——90% are passing

From the standpoint of patients, any grade below "A" is an "F"—especially if the caregiver before you is subpar. The goal is always one hundred percent. Realistically, peak performers, of course, have down moments. A-performing cultures are so strong they self-correct.

Consider Wave Theory (discussed in *Radical Loving Care*) that demonstrates that culture change is a matter of momentum. All you need is about half your group to start tipping the wave toward genuine transformation.

Why do most hospitals fail? It is because they are unable or unwilling to set a transformative vision and then to tackle the core culture issues in a tough-minded and tender-hearted way.

Mayo Clinic and the middle-sized Parrish Medical Center have something in common. They have each established caring cultures of excellence that *naturally* influence each encounter.

High performing organizations not only set love-based visions but they also focus almost obsessively on *changing the core relationships* that determine success. They understand the enormous power of *peer influence* and ensure they are hiring, training, retaining and promoting to the highest standards.

KEY: An in-house coach and/or Chief Experience Officer

Once you have gotten the message on loving care clear with your leaders, *appoint an executive to be their coach*—to reinforce the work. Reading a book or hearing a speech will never be enough. An in-house champion who teaches the work every day is crucial.

Remember the caregiver who stroked the back of the dying baby? Remember the nurse who stood up to her supervisor to take a wheelchair to a critically ill patient? Remember the heart patient who waited four days to receive help he should have gotten on the first day?

> *Let the beauty we love be what we do.*
>
> Rainer Maria Rilke

Once upon a time, when you were a little kid, you woke up sick and feverish one night. Maybe you felt so sick you thought you would die. You yearned for relief.

When your mother appeared with a cool washcloth she also brought the most healing gift in the world, love. Her caregiver presence in your childhood showed you your life had meaning.

Today, someone's mother or child or friend is coming to your hospital for care but it is for cancer treatment or a heart attack, not a mild fever. It is for a head injury that threatens their life, not a cut finger.

Sickness or injury has felled them. They are frightened as well as ill.

Can you promise each of them that everyone will give them the radical loving care you would want for your family? Patients are counting on that. Their caregivers are counting on you.

Ultimately, your decisions about your leadership are intensely personal. You have values grounded deep within you and you have decisions you make anew every day. Deep within you, as well, lie the powers we have been describing so extensively. My fondest hope for you (and the hope of all with whom you work) is that you, as the top leader in your organization will find the courage to plumb those depths. That you will be among the rare and unique people reading this book that will choose to be a real pioneer as well as a good settler.

Rilke wrote this clearly in his *Letters to a Young Poet*: "I know of no other advice than this: Go within and scale the depths of your being from which your very life springs forth." We are talking about *your* "very life." Like so much old wisdom, this advice is rarely followed. That is why radical loving leaders are so few in number.

If you do not make a *whole person* decision about your leadership, you are sure to join the crowd that walks the half-lit path to its ordinary end. Your leadership choices will reflect if you truly believe living your deepest values or if you were simply mouthing those values because they sounded right.

Is it time, now, for you to galvanize yourself and your staff around a *new* vision of healing? The Mother Test is the approach that succeeds. Is it time for you to live love, not fear? Can you lead your people forward into those "broad, sunlit uplands" Winston Churchill described, the place where love thrives?

The stakes are high. They are suffering and recovery. They are life and death.

Ultimately, the path to radical loving leadership leads to a place of mystery rather than one of certainty. Surrounded by others, you nevertheless travel with a personal vision that trumps anything written on paper.

What, really, can you do as a leader to transform the human experience? Mother Teresa suggested an answer: "What can you do to promote world peace?" she asked, "Go home and love your family."

What can you do to lead healthcare change? Go out and love those who are caring for the sick and wounded.

Radical Loving Care is the philosophy that matters. The Mother Test, and the use of every tool to support it, is the approach that works.

As Anne Sexton wrote, "Put your ear down close to your soul and listen hard." What do you hear?

In a letter to Churchill during WW II Franklin Roosevelt wrote, "It is fun to be in the same decade with you."

Roosevelt cherished and admired Churchill and Churchill felt the same about Roosevelt. A canticle of gratitude sang through both their hearts. These two beings knew that they had, more than any others, saved a way of life for all who followed them. These two ordinary people lived radical loving leadership.

Franklin Roosevelt's older cousin, Theodore, described his years as President as his "crowded hours." In fact, he packed more action into his Presidency than most of his predecessors engaged in their entire lives.

The boldest thing this book calls you to do is to engage love's power in your work, to honor your leadership as a sacred trust, to climb into the arms of Lincoln's better angels and be a lover.

We end where we began.

There's an old woman down the hall. She calls to you. She has cancer. You can hide or you can answer. Or you can ride the wings of angels and be a lover.

Pass The Mother Test and you will pass The Leader Test—and your life test. Listen to Yoda. "Do or do not. There is no try."

Start now.

Your mother is counting on you.

Epilogue

On May 23, 2015, John Forbes Nash, Jr. and his wife were riding in a taxicab when the driver lost control. The Nashes died in the crash.

Nash was profiled in Ron Howard's film "A Beautiful Mind." He was revered as a math genius and awarded the Nobel Memorial Prize for Economics. He suffered from paranoid schizophrenia. For a long time, his life centered on the mathematical sciences and that is where he sought answers to earth's conundrums. Towards the end of his life, Nash found a different pathway to truth. He wrote, "I've always believed in numbers. In the equations and logics that lead to reason. But after a lifetime of such pursuits, I ask, what truly is logic? Who decides reason?"

We all ask these questions at some moment in our lives and often give up. Nash never did. He passes on to us what he learned in his eighty-six years: "My quest has taken me through the physical, the metaphysical, the delusional, and back — and I have made the most important discovery of my career — the most important discovery of my life: It is only in the mysterious equations of love that any logic or reasons can be found."

If Nash, an atheist and skeptic as well as a genius, could reach such a conclusion what does it tell us? How do you and I calculate the importance of "the mysterious equations of love?"

One late spring day in Sherborne, Massachusetts, I witnessed a variation on love's "mysterious equations." A divine dawn broke both night's hold and my heart. Above me, the May light sewed a hundred gold scarves & tossed them into the woods lassoing the grateful necks of the tallest oaks. One scarf dressed a female gingko in pale chiffon dotted with shape-shifting shadows.

Later, I visited the 19th century home of landscape genius Frederick Law Olmsted (creator of Central Park). Near the hem of his yard, I watched the mid-afternoon sun trim the tips of a choir of Bleeding Hearts.

There was joy. There was pain. There was mystery. All loving care is like this.

Why must love demand so much of us? Why can't we limit love's divine magic so that it is all joy and no sorrow?

The key to our humanity is secreted in this conundrum. Nash experienced it. So have you. He spent his life, "always believing in numbers..." So do so many leaders I know, never seeming to understand that the most important truths lie far beyond hard calculations. Toward his end, Nash finally glimpsed the fact that it is love that crowns life's hierarchy of values.

In the new land of artificial intelligence scientists create robots that do fantastical things. One thing robots will not experience is suffering. What inventor would program that awful feeling into a machine? Neither will anyone be able to conjure compassion into computers that are, by definition, heartless.

Robots can only mimic. In the comment section of the *Journal of Sacred Work* a person who only identifies himself as "JVD" wrote: "A robot is the sum of someone's numbers. But the Divine is infinite." John O'Donohue offered another observation that affirms every caregiver, "The ability to care is the hallmark of the human, the touchstone of morality and the ground of holiness," he wrote. "Without the warmth of care, the world becomes a graveyard. In the kindness of care, the divine comes alive in us."

Where do we witness love's mysteries? How do we discern love's meaning in our lives? At his fourth birthday my youngest grandson coughed. Glancing around the table he announced, "Hey everyone, the Birthday Boy coughed!" In that divinely funny moment, he felt regal and affirmed. So did we. What he knew was that we cared. What we all felt was the magic of the divine.

I hope he will discover sooner than Nash that numbers are useful. And also that, "It is only in the mysterious equations of love that any logic or reasons can be found."

Maybe this is why I love the way poets, Tennyson and Dickinson, for example, arranged words into lines that frame our quests for life and heaven. They are among the many disciples that send us their love. Their ghosts join all the Radical Loving Leaders in offering you inspiration and solace on this day in your own life journey.

...*The long day wanes; the slow moon climbs; the deep*
Moans round with many voices. Come, my friends.
'Tis not too late to seek a newer world.

Push off, and sitting well in order smite

the sounding furrows; for my purpose holds
To sail beyond the sunset, and the baths
Of all the western stars, until I die.
It may be that the gulfs will wash us down;
It may be that we shall touch the Happy Isles,
And see the great Achilles, whom we knew.
Though much is taken, much abides; and though
We are not now that strength which in old days
Moved earth and heaven, that which we are, we are---
One equal temper of heroic hearts,
Made weak by time and fate, but strong in will
To strive, to seek, to find, and not to yield.

-from *Ulysses*, by Alfred, Lord Tennyson - 1842

How excellent the heaven,
When earth cannot be had;
How hospitable, then, the face
of our old neighbor, God!

Emily Dickinson

Note and Disclaimer

This is a storybook not a textbook. The reports and counsel written her are offered to inspire you, as a leader, in your work guiding others.

The stories told in this book are grounded in my best recollections and observations. In most cases they are inspired by true events but many names have been changed and stories may combine elements from different experiences. Statistics are offered from recollection rather than research. Each story is true in spirit if not in every fact.

There is no intention to unfairly harm or embarrass any specific person or organization, but only to honor the precepts of loving leadership.

Erie Chapman Foundation is solely responsible for the content of this book and is the recipient of proceeds from sales.

"Erie Chapman" by Arnold Newman, 1994

About The Author

Erie Chapman's half-century career reflects the life of a renaissance man. His leadership experience began early. He served as Student Body President in both high school and at Northwestern University.

At age nineteen he was diagnosed with Crohn's disease. Against his doctor's advice, he continued to pursue an aggressive career.

TOLEDO:

Mr. Chapman began as a trial attorney with Eastman and Smith in Toledo. In 1972 at twenty-nine, he was appointed a Federal Prosecutor with the U.S. Department of Justice.

Three years later Mr. Chapman was recruited to run Riverside, a 271-bed inner city Episcopal hospital. He became President and CEO in 1977 at thirty-three and led an organization with two thousand employees and three hundred physicians to continuously higher levels of success. He founded the first hospital-based health promotion center, built peak patient satisfaction scores and was named Toledo's Outstanding Young Man of the Year.

In 1976 Chapman was also appointed a part time Acting Judge of The Sylvania Municipal Court, a position he held until 1982 when he was appointed to a similar position in Perrysburg, Ohio.

COLUMBUS:

In 1983, at age thirty-nine, Mr. Chapman took over Ohio's largest hospital, 1000 bed Riverside Methodist, in Columbus, Ohio. In his first year he established Hospice at Riverside. During his twelve-year tenure patient satisfaction rose from the 68th to the 98th percentile and income steadily increased from $2 million dollars to $56 million dollars. Mr. Chapman led significant advancements in clinical excellence through his establishment of the Riverside Heart Institute, The Riverside Center for Women's Health and the Riverside Cancer Institute.

In 1990 Riverside Methodist joined The Mayo Clinic and Boston's Beth Israel Hospital as one of the top three service-oriented hospitals in America. (*Service America*) In 1992 Riverside was named one of the top 10 most employee friendly workplaces in the nation on the ABC television series, "Revolution at Work." *Working Mother Magazine* named Riverside one of the nation's best places to work. Erie Chapman was singled out as one of America's most innovative CEOs in the 1996 book *Reaching for the Stars.*

In 1984 Chapman founded the OhioHealth Corporation out of Riverside. Across his presidency OhioHealth became a ten-hospital system and continues to this day as one of the most successful healthcare systems in the country.

FORT LAUDERDALE:

In 1995 Mr. Chapman joined InPhynet Medical Management, a publicly traded company based in Fort Lauderdale, Florida. Over the next two years, he helped lead the company successfully until, at its peak, it was sold to healthcare giant MedPartners.

NASHVILLE:

In 1998 Mr. Chapman became President and CEO of Baptist Hospital System, Nashville's largest. He led the organization through a $74 million dollar turnaround in just three years. Under his leadership, patient satisfaction rose from the low seventies to the high nineties. Clinical excellence strengthened in women's health, heart, orthopedics and cancer. Employee satisfaction rose into the nineties while turnover dropped into single digits as Baptist became an employee friendly workplace.

Mr. Chapman became founding President and CEO of the $140 million Baptist Healing Hospital Trust in 2002. Under his leadership the Trust gave millions of dollars in grants to area charities over the next eight years.

COMMUNITY SERVICE:

In Toledo Mr. Chapman was Co-Chair of the Arts Commission and successfully championed the city's 1% for the arts legislation. He also served as a Volunteer Probation office with the Juvenile Court for four years.

In Columbus he was Chair of the United Way Campaign, Vice Chair of the Columbus Chamber of Commerce and founder of City Year Columbus, part of the Americorp initiative. He has served on more than twenty boards of for profit and non-profit organizations.

In Nashville he has become a philanthropist and, through Erie Chapman Foundation has helped contribute to and serve dozens of Tennessee charities.

TELEVISION and RADIO:

Mr. Chapman's career includes eight years as founder and host of "Life Choices with Erie Chapman" a television show syndicated in 110 cities and 22 foreign countries. He won two regional Emmys for his work. Simultaneously, he hosted "Sports Health Live" on WBNS radio.

THE ARTS:

WRITING: Mr. Chapman is the author of the best-selling book, *Radical Loving Care*. Also, *Sacred Work*, *The Caregiver Meditations*, *Inside Radical Loving Care* and a children's book, *Scotty The Snail*. He edits and is a weekly columnist for the online weblog, *The Journal of Sacred Work*.

PHOTOGRAPHY: An Award-winning photographer, Erie's images have been exhibited in New York at the Union League Gallery, at The Toledo Museum of Art, at the Wustum Gallery in Wisconsin, The Edison Gallery and at The Halstead Gallery in Ann Arbor, Michigan.

POETRY: His poetry has been published nationally and in the book *Woman As Beauty* under the name Dane Dakota.

MUSIC: He co-composed the music for four albums including a piano concerto (with Mark Volker) released in 2010.

DOCUMENTARY FILM: He produced and created four documentary films including "Acts of Caring," the highly successful "Sacred Work," "The Servant's Heart" and "A Place Called Alive."

FEATURE FILMS, PLAYS and SHORT FILMS: Under the name Dane Dakota, Mr. Chapman wrote the play "Who Loves Judas?" which premiered in Tennessee and Florida in 2009. He produced and created two award-winning feature films, "Who Loves Judas?" and "Alex Dreaming" (which won Best Picture awards in Atlanta and Memphis film festivals.) He also produced, created, and directed the short film "Amies Nues" released in 2014.

MINISTRY:

Erie Chapman graduated from Vanderbilt Divinity School in 2002 and was ordained in 2009. He ministers to inmates on Tennessee's Death Row.

EDUCATION:

Mr. Chapman holds a Bachelor of Science Degree from Northwestern University, a Juris Doctor degree from George Washington University Law School, and a Masters in Theological Studies degree from Vanderbilt.

TODAY:

Erie Chapman serves as President of Chapman Health International, Dane Dakota Productions and Erie Chapman Foundation. He consults regularly with hospitals, hospices, and other charities and is the founding editor of *Journal of Sacred Work*.

He has been married since 1966 and has two children and four grandchildren.

SELECTED TESTIMONIALS

"Erie Chapman has described the special qualities that separate the great from the good among people and in organizations. *What a different place the world would be if we could all live out his healing model.*"

Mike Means, past President and CEO,
Health First, Melbourne, FL

"Erie helps us understand that we need to be radical, loving, caring people who transform and heal our society."

Lloyd Dean, President and CEO,
Dignity Health System, San Francisco

"Erie Chapman has demonstrated extraordinary leadership in healthcare." –

Martha Marsh, past President and CEO,
Stanford Hospitals and Clinics, Palo Alto

"Anyone who leads a healthcare organization of any kind should read *Radical Loving Care*."

> Chuck Lauer, publisher,
> *Modern Healthcare* magazine

"Through *Radical Loving Care*, Erie Chapman offers a concept of humanism that sets a new standard."

> Dr. Thomas Chapman (no relation) past President and CEO,
> HSC Foundation, Washington, D.C.

"Erie Chapman delivers a clarion call to action by reminding all of us that *we must nurture the soul as well as treat the body* if we are to be true healers. He not only provides a concise blueprint for how hospitals can achieve 'loving care' but also demonstrates how it makes good business sense to do so."

> Ed Eckenoff, past President and CEO,
> National Rehabilitation Hospital Network

"Ensuring that each patient and caregiver, without exception, receives loving care in every encounter is a radical idea that is long overdue. Erie Chapman has made believers of our Board, Medical Staff, Associates and Volunteers."

> Dennis Swan, President and CEO,
> Sparrow Hospital System, Lansing, MI

"Bravo to Erie Chapman for his astounding leadership and unparalleled assault on the status quo. His efforts will transform healthcare into something truly better for all Americans."

> Gerry Mayo, former Chairman,
> The Midland Insurance Company

"He is a true renaissance man."

> Jeff Kaplan, former Associate Vice Provost,
> Vanderbilt University

Continued on back cover.

CPSIA information can be obtained at www.ICGtesting.com
Printed in the USA
LVOW07s0031070715

445107LV00002B/2/P